From Corporate Greed To Common Good

Canadian Churches and Community Economic Development

Edited by Murray MacAdam
with John Bird and Kevin Arsenault

NOVALIS

Behold, I make all things new.
Revelation 21:5

© 1998 Novalis, Saint Paul University, Ottawa, Canada
Cover: Blair Turner Communication Design Inc.
Layout: Chris Humphrey

Novalis Business Offices
49 Front St. East, Second Floor
Toronto, Ontario
M5E 1B3
1-800-387-7164 or (416) 363-3303

To contact the editor, Murray MacAdam, about community economic development, please e-mail him at macadam@web.net.

The Scripture quotations in the Introduction are from the New Revised Standard
Version Bible, © 1989, and the Scripture quotations elsewhere are from the Revised Standard Version Bible, © 1966, both by the Division of Christian Education of the National Council of the Churches of Christ in the U.S.A. Used by
permission.

Canadian Cataloguing-in-Publication Data
From corporate greed to common good: Canadian churches and community
economic development
Includes bibliographical references.
ISBN 2-89088-844-4
1. Community economic development–Religious aspects–Christianity.
2. Economic development projects–Canada. I. Arsenault, Kevin J. II. Bird, John
III. MacAdam, Murray
BR115.E3F76 1998   261.8'5'0971   C98-901174-7

Printed in Canada

*To David Walsh
and David Peters-Woods*

for keeping hope alive

CONTRIBUTORS

KEVIN ARSENAULT is a member of the Cooper Institute and is president of Rural Dignity of Canada. He operates a consulting company, Rural Information Services, in his native Prince Edward Island. Kevin was executive director of the Jesuit Centre for Social Faith and Justice, and has also worked for the National Farmers Union.

ED BENNETT and DIANNE HEISE live on a farm with their family in Perth County, Ontario, and are neighbours with the Old Order Amish. Ed is a professor of psychology at Wilfrid Laurier University and has done community development work for over 30 years. Dianne is a homemaker and president of the Milverton-Morningtion Economic Development Corporation.

JOHN BIRD is a writer for *The United Church Observer*. He has written for many publications and is the co-author, with Diane Engelstad, of *Nation to Nation: Aboriginal Sovereignty and the Future of Canada*. John has worked for the Anglican Church of Canada and Citizens for Public Justice. He lives in Bobcaygeon, Ontario.

MURRAY MACADAM works for a community economic development project in Toronto's Jane-Finch neighbourhood. A long-time writer and social activist, he has worked for the Anglican Church of Canada, World Vision and Citizens for Public Justice. Murray was editor of the CED newsletter *Community Economics* from 1991-1996. He's the author of *Making Waves: The Grindstone Story*. He can be reached at macadam@web.net.

Fr. GREG MACLEOD has more than 20 years of experience in community economic development as founding chair of New Dawn Enterprises and of BCA Holdings, a community-based venture capital finance company. He has led study tours to Mondragon, Spain, and is author of *From Mondragon to America*. A professor

iv

of philosophy at the University College of Cape Breton, he lives in Sydney, Nova Scotia.

CYNTHIA PATTERSON lives in Barachois de Malbaie, a fishing and forestry village on the Gaspé Peninsula. A co-founder of Rural Dignity, she also serves on the executive of the Council of Canadians and on the Ecojustice Committee of the Anglican Church of Canada.

LAURA REILLY is a homemaker who lives with her family in Stratford, Ontario. She's an active supporter of her local Fair Share Harvest program, writes for *Catholic New Times* and is active in her parish.

JANET SOMERVILLE is general secretary of the Canadian Council of Churches. A veteran journalist, she has written for many publications and was associate editor of *Catholic New Times* for many years. She lives in Toronto.

ACKNOWLEDGEMENTS

This book would not have been possible without support from a wide range of individuals and church groups. Financial support from the following groups was crucial: The Urban Mission Fund of the Anglican Diocese of Toronto, the Church of the Redeemer, the Canadian Conference of Catholic Bishops, Phoenix Community Works Foundation and the DJT Foundation. We thank those who made individual donations.

Many individuals provided helpful information, agreed to be interviewed or helped in other ways. Special thanks to Ann Abraham, Marvin Anderson, Gregory Baum, Paul Born, Andrew Brouwer, Beth Coates, Lee Davis Creal, Linda Donville, Eugene Ellmen, Cornelius Guenter, Dwayne Hodgson, Brian Iler, Ann Keating, Harry Kits, Cathy Lang, Jim MacDonald, Lynn Markell, Jim Marshall, Ruth Morris, Barb Paleczny, David Pell, Charles Purdy, Allan Reeve, Carol Reeve, Larry Rooney, Mark Vandervennen and David Walsh.

A special thanks to Rosie and Ruth for their patience.

The two articles on community-shared agriculture in Chapter 10 first appeared in *Catholic New Times,* December 1, 1996. Reprinted with permission.

Some of the material on the Anglican Community Development Fund in Chapter 8 first appeared in *The Anglican.* Reprinted with permission.

This book is one of the final projects undertaken by the Jesuit Centre for Social Faith and Justice, which closed in July 1997.

CONTENTS

Contributors iv

1. Introduction 1
   Janet Somerville

2. Community Economic Development in Canada:
   Band-Aid or Breakthrough? 11
   Murray MacAdam

3. Babylon Revisited:
   CED and the Economic Injustice of Our Times 29
   Kevin Arsenault

4. New Dawn:
   The Cape Breton Giant 46
   John Bird

5. Edmonton Recycling Society:
   Mixing a Mission with Bottom-line Success 57
   John Bird

6. Getting the Church Onside:
   Riverdale Economic Ministry 66
   Murray MacAdam

7. Kagiwiosa Manomin:
   A First-Nation CED Project 74
   John Bird

8. Up and Over the Money Wall..83
    Murray MacAdam

9. Mondragon:
    Ideas with Legs..94
    Greg MacLeod

10. Fair Shares for Farmers:
    Community-Shared Agriculture......................................106
    Edward M. Bennett and Dianne Heise

    An Advent Reflection from a Fair Share Family............114
    Laura Reilly

11. Growing the Community Economy..............................117
    Murray MacAdam

    Afterword..131
    Cynthia Patterson

    Resources..147

CHAPTER 1

Introduction

JANET SOMERVILLE

When you have come into the land that the Lord your God is giving you as an inheritance to possess, and you possess it, and settle in it, you shall take some of the first of all the fruit of the ground which you harvest from the land that the Lord your God is giving you, and you shall put it in a basket and go . . . to the priest who is in office at that time, and say to him, "Today I declare to the Lord your God that I have come into the land that the Lord swore to our ancestors to give us."

When the priest takes the basket from your hand and sets it down before the altar of the Lord your God, you shall make this response before the Lord your God: "A wandering Aramean was my ancestor; he went down into Egypt and lived there as an alien, few in number, and there he became a great nation, mighty and populous. When the Egyptians treated us harshly and afflicted us, by imposing hard labour on us, we cried to the Lord, the God of our ancestors. The Lord heard our voice and saw our affliction, our toil and our oppression. The Lord brought us out of Egypt with a mighty hand and an outstretched arm, with a terrifying display of power, and with signs and wonders. He brought us into this place and gave us this land, a land flowing with milk and honey. So now I bring the first fruit of the ground that you, O Lord, have given me."

You shall set it down before the Lord your God and bow down before the Lord your God. Then you, together with the Levites and the aliens who reside among you, shall celebrate with all the bounty that the Lord your God has given to you and to your house.

Deuteronomy 26:1–11

Christians often grow up with an exceedingly unbiblical vision of what redemption is about. Somehow we come to assume that the saving work of God is directed only at "souls."

It's not that our basic faith-symbols get it wrong. We acknowledge that God in Christ has overcome the power of sin and death, which had human history in its grip. We teach that God's own communal life, the very source of love and of justice and of the breath-taking beauty of Creation, has been poured forth into human hearts as a free gift. We baptize people into this awesome mystery of new life.

But then we timidly limit our expectations of what that gift of new life might do. We don't often teach our children that God's life, working in them and in us, will challenge and transform the structures that control so much of everyday living for all human beings—the structures of the economy, for example. We somehow think that grace will change our "hearts," but won't change the reality of economic life. This reality, we think, must remain cold, greedy and ruled by a calculus of domination which is the very opposite of neighbourly love.

Wherever that impression comes from, it certainly doesn't come from a careful reading of Scripture.

The Biblical Paradigm

For the Bible, the very paradigm of salvation is the redemption from slavery in Egypt. That mighty work wasn't merely a negative breakthrough, a saving *from* alienated work. It led, through risk

2

and supreme effort and bone-deep, struggling faith, to a life so precious that it was like a re-founding of Creation, like a recovery of Eden. It led to the gift of a land "flowing with milk and honey." It led to a generous, egalitarian economy shaped by laws that ranked neighbourly and family solidarity far, far ahead of profit-taking. It led to reverence for a particular environment—contemplative gratitude for land understood not as a commodity but as a gift from God, an inheritance, a family vocation. It led from bureaucratized supply management (remember those storehouse-cities the Hebrews built for the pharaohs in Egypt?) to face-to-face sharing. It led from elitist control of the labour force and of all the means of production to an amazingly decentralized pattern of ownership and responsibility.

You could sum it up by saying that the first great act of divine redemption—the one announced in the call to Moses from the burning bush—led from an imperial economy to a neighbourly economy. More precisely, it led to the revelation that a neighbourly economy is possible, and is what we truly need. And that a neighbourly economy is always fragile. Why? Because it can be sustained only in freedom, and only by peaceful hearts converted to neighbourly love. This book is full of stories about people who understand that in every generation, an "economic exodus," like the one Moses began in his time, is both possible and necessary.

And difficult. No kind of conversion is more difficult than economic conversion, no vocation more challenging. In every generation, the invitation to build an economy that incarnates the revolutionary divine law—*you shall love your neighbour as yourself*—is an act of defiance of the dominant economy which everywhere incarnates our "fallen-ness."

The stories told in this book are true stories about people who refuse to separate economics from community. From loving one's neighbour as oneself. And from caring about the earth under one's feet.

These days, the movement supported by people who want to build a neighbourly economy is often called "community economic development." (The same idea gets different names at different moments; in my father's youth, it was called "the co-operative movement.")

People involved in community economic development are quite aware that they are defying the dominant trend in today's world. From the point of view of the implacable, idolatrous and brilliantly-informed reasoning that makes the "global free market" sound so logical and sophisticated, these neighbour-loving locals are heretics.

I love the story in Chapter 4 that describes a prelude to one of the New Dawn undertakings in Cape Breton. The setting is Sydney, with its cripplingly high unemployment rate. The Scotia Rope plant—set up with generous dollops of taxpayers' money—has just closed, laying off one hundred percent of its workers. The "owners," declaring the company bankrupt, have sold the assets to an American company which plans to truck the machinery and parts all the way to Louisiana.

Except the trucks can't get to the plant. Why? All these Cape Breton church ladies are blocking the way with their bodies, that's why. So are union members and the odd clergyman. But I'll bet it was the church ladies who bewildered the truckers and paralyzed the local police. Who would have expected the mothers of the tribe to be on the front lines of such a display of communal defiance?

There's another story I love, in Chapter 11. It's about defiance too, but a much more polite form of it. The setting is Edmonton, and the project is the establishment of a restaurant—in City Hall, no less—that will preferentially employ street youth who have come to the point of wanting to learn job-market skills. But a newly elected City Council is balking at the idea of sharing their prestigious work space with such disreputable workers. Locate the project somewhere else, says the new mayor.

What happened then? The visionaries who had launched the idea—an initiative of the Edmonton City Centre Church Corporation—went back to their congregations and said: "This is about who gets to be considered a member of the community, and who gets excluded. Young people in trouble are members of our community. They are our kids, like it or not. Keeping them out of

City Hall is a deliberate choice to keep them marginalized. And that's evil."

Hundreds of phone calls with some variant of that message proceeded to flow in to the elected councillors. The mayor was embarrassed. The restaurant project went ahead—in City Hall, as proposed.

Working and Dwelling Locally

If any of your kin fall into difficulty and become depen-
dent on you . . . you shall not make them serve as slaves.
They shall remain with you as hired or bound labourers.
They shall serve with you until the year of the jubilee.
Then they and their children with them shall be free from
your authority; they shall . . . return to their ancestral
property. For they are my servants, whom I brought out
of the land of Egypt; they shall not be sold as slaves are
sold. You shall not rule over them with harshness, but
shall fear your God.

Leviticus 25:35–43

In the biblical vision of a redeemed economy, it is taken for granted that a free community does its own work. The neighbourhood grows and shares its own food, tends to its own flocks, weaves its own cloth, sews its own clothes, and builds its own dwellings. What is surplus can safely be sold out of the community, but what is essential should be provided from within. That is the way of *shalom*. Work should be seen and honoured within the solidarity of neighbourliness. Normally, work should not simply be "paid for" in an indifferent, anonymous transaction.

Of course the understanding of "neighbourhood" changes in a world where we can all get around faster than the speed of sound, where we can have live conversations that span thousands of miles, where we can exchange bookfuls of information in microseconds without leaving our own offices. But technology doesn't change everything about human reality. Internet access doesn't suddenly blot out our local obligations. We still need to live a life of mutual responsibility where we physically dwell.

Good, local work is visible, transparent, accountable. It is generative of neighbourliness. Better than that: good local work is *revelatory*. Through it, people come to understand their own earth, their own resources, their own communal possibilities, the very meaning of Creation in their locality. You can feel the conviction about local work shining through the Community-Shared Agriculture project that is described in Chapter 10. There, food is not merely bought and sold. A shared responsibility is acknowledged for good stewardship of the local earth. Visits are exchanged. Bonds are forged between farmers and eaters. Mutual understanding is cultivated along with the cabbages and carrots. "Best buy" is not equivalent to "cheapest."

City-born Laura Reilly writes in Chapter 10 of her initiation into a harvest-sharing partnership with Amish farm families dwelling near her town. Her words are an evocative description of a covenant economy. Her joy is an invitation to try something like community-shared agriculture where you live.

Stratford, where the Reillys live, is a small city. The distance to their Amish neighbours is not prohibitive. Yet in a community economic development project in the relatively big city of Edmonton, you can glimpse exactly the same recovery of neighbourliness, the same refusal of anonymity.

The Edmonton Recycling Society, described in Chapter 5, does the unglamorous work of picking up and processing household recyclables. Most of its employees arrive wearing the official label of being "severely employment-disadvantaged." Yet their company has established stability and won expanding contracts as a worker-governed, non-profit corporation.

The executive director of Edmonton Recycling says that the key is simple: treat workers as members of an extended family. "We stand with each other whenever we possibly can," says Cornelius Guenter.

Creation and Community

Good human relations is not the only issue the Edmonton group cares about, though. Their "family" spirit is woven into a bigger belief in Creation and mission. They believe in recycling not merely as a business opportunity but as an act of stewardship within Creation. For them, local economic development is not only a "niche market," but an assertion of commitment to a neighbourly life.

Even deeper convictions about Creation and community can be glimpsed in other stories in this book. Under the difficult struggle to sustain a wild rice gathering and marketing company in northern Ontario (see Chapter 7) runs the dark river of imperial history. All the indigenous economies on this half of the North American continent were colonized by a globally dominant imperial economy—or rather, by two of them, one British and one French. Between them (and in bloody competition with each other) they "opened up" what is now Canada. But in doing so the colonizers scorned the deep sense of place that anchored local societies. They shredded rights and traditions that gave resonant meaning to the daily work of North America's indigenous people.

So when Joe Pitchenese tries to revive his Anishinaabe people's care for the wild rice beds in their traditional territory (*manomin* is the Ojibway word for the plant—it means "Seed of the Great Spirit"), he is struggling for more than the survival of a co-op in a capitalist environment. He is aiming for the recovery of identity, of culture, of resourcefulness, of joy in work. He is fighting for a future in which his people will again have a right relationship to Creation in their own locality. "When the Anishinaabe people treat the manomin with proper respect," he tells the Canadian Wild Rice Council, "the manomin responds by giving itself up for the sustenance and livelihood of the people."

That's mysticism, of a good and healthy kind. It's deeply related to work and to a sense of place. I'm sure St. Benedict, with his convictions about work and prayer and his vow of monastic stability (talk about a sense of place!) would have approved heartily of Joe Pitchenese.

7

Community economic development, if it succeeds in getting breathing and growing space, will require that we recognize again that human communities have rights that are more important than the "rights" of rootless money.

A settled human community has an intrinsic right to use the natural resources in its own locality, so that it can meet its own needs and live gratefully and industriously in its own place. This right runs deeper than the right of restless global capital (or in the bad old days, of imperial troops) to swoop in and "buy" (or conquer) land and resources. The point of being sons and daughters of Adam and Eve is to *dwell* somewhere—to dwell *together* in a place experienced as a gift/trust from the Creator—and to use the resources of that place to meet the needs of all who dwell there. This is intrinsic to the human vocation in a Creation that was intended to be a Garden of Eden, a place of *shalom*.

Global profit-hunters restlessly move factories from one continent to another, hunting for the cheapest possible hourly wage and the least demanding work force. Have technology, will travel, want money. What has any of that got to do with the human vocation to dwell lovingly together in a place where you can put down deep roots? What does it have to do with joy, finally?

Without joy in work, you're not going to get a lot of joy in life. In many of the stories in this book, those who take action are feeling an urgency to make joy possible by restoring, at least for a few people at a time, the possibility of joy in work.

That's why this is a book about joy, though the stories are sometimes stories of failure.

Planting Good Seed

The truth is that we won't live to see a perfect economy functioning in this world, or even in one neighbourhood. Neither will our children. There is simply too much hardness in our own hearts, and too much "fallen-ness" in the interlocking layers of human history, to produce perfection in the work of our hands and brains. A perfectly neighbourly economy remains a vision of the end-time—as Micah puts it so succinctly, of a time when "nation shall not lift up sword against nation, neither shall they learn war any more; but they shall all sit under their own vines and under their own fig trees, and no one shall make them afraid, for the mouth of the Lord of hosts has spoken" (Micah 4:4).

But that doesn't at all mean that efforts towards a covenant economy make no real difference, or that they are unimportant. They are intensely important. They are a crucial dimension of the bearing of faith-witness in this world. They are fruitful out of all proportion to their size. And because this kind of neighbourly, creation-respecting economy is so truly human, even fragile and fragmentary examples of it *begin to give joy as soon as they are seriously attempted.*

We live in a deeply idolatrous world, and we are all products of that world as well as being "children of light." The parables of Jesus make it clear that in the fields of such a world, weeds and wheat grow up together. It's presumptuous to try to exterminate all the weeds right now, in the belief that we will be left with God's pure wheat. The actual, functioning economy will always be a very mixed bag—an experience of living inside "the body of this death," as Paul says so dramatically.

Yet with our own work, with our own money, we can and must plant good seed. We can build elements of healthy, responsive, neighbourly economies wherever we are, in all the surprising ways that we can. If we can't do it perfectly and securely, let's at least do it daringly. And with zest.

Some of us will do it by following an inner call (or the call of our neighbours in need) towards a life-work that embodies Eden rather than Babylon—to borrow Kevin Arsenault's evocative use of that biblical image. Others might support the growth of neighbourly economies by lending their money in non-conventional, hopeful ways. You'll notice that a big concern in the chapters that follow is the question of how to get things started—how to find the money for a "launch." And you'll see that there are already many interesting answers to the question, "Where can we find a sympathetic investor?"

9

Lending money generously, without too much calculation of personal profit, has been a central command of covenant economies from the earliest times. Here, as a closing thought, is the delightfully graphic opinion of the book of Deuteronomy on the subject of loans in a neighbourly economy:

> *If there is among you anyone in need, a member of your community in any of your towns within the land that the Lord your God is giving you, do not be hard-hearted or tight-fisted toward your needy neighbour. You should rather open your hands, willingly lending enough to meet the need, whatever it may be.*
>
> *Be careful that you do not entertain a mean thought, thinking, "The seventh year, the year of remission (of debts) is near," and therefore view your needy neighbour with hostility and give nothing. Your neighbour might cry to the Lord against you, and you would incur guilt. Give liberally and be ungrudging when you do so, for on this account the Lord your God will bless you in all your work and in all that you undertake.*

> Deuteronomy 15:7–12

CHAPTER 2

Community Economic Development in Canada: Band-Aid or Breakthrough?

MURRAY MACADAM

The bottom line of community economic development is neighbourly economics, as Janet Somerville notes. But what exactly does that mean? What form does a neighbourly economy take? How is this kind of economy different from the mainstream economy? Is CED destined to remain on the margins of Canada's economy?

In answering these questions, this chapter outlines how community-based economic development has, in effect, redefined economics. Indeed, CED stands traditional economics on its head. As Joan Kuyek claims, it represents an effort "to reclaim and re-name economics for ourselves." This means a neighbourly adaptation of the original meaning of economics—care of the household. Those most affected by economic decisions need to have a voice in those decisions. The decisions themselves need to stretch the boundaries of economic criteria beyond bottom-line thinking to include social and community needs as well.

Getting a business up and running is not easy, especially when you're barely making ends meet. Just ask Romeo Zapata of Winnipeg.

Zapata lost his job in the summer of 1992. While collecting unemployment insurance, he had a brain wave for a business idea. "People are interested in recycling," he says. "What else can be recycled?" Answer: printer ribbons for computers, by re-inking them. Zapata found that re-inked ribbons can be used another eight to ten times, and only cost half as much as new ones.

A great idea—except that Zapata needed business training and money for inking machines. How could someone in his position get either?

SEED Winnipeg stepped in to make the difference. SEED stands for Supporting Employment and Economic Development. Set up to help low-income people get started in business, SEED Winnipeg was launched by the Mennonite Central Committee, the Assiniboine Credit Union and the Community Education Development Association. Providing business loans and training are the two linchpins of SEED Winnipeg. Romeo Zapata received both in 1993. He hasn't looked back since.

Roofers, renovators, couriers, auto body repair—people who had been unemployed or on welfare are now working in these and many other fields, with help from SEED Winnipeg. In all, about a hundred Winnipeg-area people are now working in their own businesses after being helped by the organization.

The help extends well beyond a rigorous training program and a loan program offering loans of up to $10,000. Business mentors from the Mennonite Economic Development Association provide advice and moral support, especially during the critical and often difficult early days of a new business.

SEED Winnipeg changed from a nice idea to a living reality thanks in large part to the credit union, which agreed to put $100,000 into the program, and under easier loan terms than those faced by most borrowers.

This innovative job-creation venture springs from the values of the Mennonites who support it. "Our vision for humanity, of the *shalom* community, is a vision of enabling people to live as fully as possible," says Mennonite Central Committee employment director Garry Loewen. "Poverty prevents people from living life fully. A just society is one where the system is not so brutal to a large segment of the population."

The Co-operative Capital of North America

The weather didn't co-operate for the big event: –20° C in April 1990. Yet that didn't really matter. Everyone—or it seemed liked everyone—in the Evangeline region of Prince Edward Island was too excited to care about cold weather at a time like this. A new, co-operatively owned supermarket was opening, and that had people fired up. But it wasn't just any supermarket: it was their supermarket, owned jointly by all its customers. Eight hundred people turned out to mark the occasion—in an area with only 2,500 residents.

At the opening ceremony, Rev. Eloi Arsenault, a Catholic priest serving the community and a strong co-op supporter, stressed the role that co-operatives have always played in the lives of Evangeline people. Its sixteen co-operatives make up the lifeblood of the area, employing 350 people, or one person in every two households. Co-operative enterprises have been set up to provide health care, housing, nursing care, crafts, tourism, funeral services and even cable TV. Indeed, this area has been described as "the uncontested co-operative capital of North America" (Jack Quarter, *Building a Community Controlled Economy*, 1996, 3).

As citizens of a province where jobs are scarce, the residents of Evangeline have not been afraid to start new co-operative businesses in order to create work. They formed three co-ops between 1962 and 1973. Since 1977 they've launched fourteen more. Not all have survived. But most have, providing an example of how communities can take matters into their own hands and succeed.

A Business Incubator

"This is like my second home," says Lee Champion, gesturing to the small room around her. Bolts of cloth and fabric lie scattered about, the tools of her trade as an interior designer. It's a small room, but it suits Champion's needs. Besides, here at the York Business Opportunity Centre, there's much more to help her meet other business needs: office, accounting, legal and other services.

The centre, housed in a sprawling former warehouse in the Metro Toronto community of York, works with prospective entrepreneurs through all phases of the business start-up cycle. At any one time, about twelve to fifteen businesses like Lee Champion's are being nurtured in it. Some new entrepreneurs remain at the Business Opportunity Centre for as little as six months, while most stay for two or three years.

Lee Champion has called the York Business Opportunity Centre home for four years. It's a good arrangement for her, one that's enabled her to build up her business over the years. Marketing advice from the Centre has made a big difference.

Being a business "incubator," hatching the eggs of business dreams into living, breeding businesses, is only part of what happens at this business centre. People come for an hour or two of advice on starting their business. Others come for in-depth self-employment training offered through the federally funded Self-Employment Assistance program. It lets unemployment insurance recipients continue receiving benefits while they learn about starting a business.

There's still more magic happening in the old warehouse housing the York Business Opportunity Centre. Walking along one of its hallways, you're likely to come upon a group of immigrant women listening to a teacher during an English language class. The fact that their children are being cared for next door in a daycare centre is a godsend to these women. Another bend in the hallway and you glimpse a group of people hunched over computer keyboards, intent on learning a new program. At lunch-time, you can be served with enthusiasm by an apprentice cook in the cafeteria.

It's all part of the balanced recipe for nurturing community economic development offered by the Learning Enrichment Foundation, a social agency on the front lines of economic change. The foundation is the umbrella organization for the York Business Opportunity Centre and a variety of other community services.

York, where the centre is located, is where the recession hits reality—*hard*. An older, heavily immigrant and blue-collar area, it's been battered by plant closures. The Learning Enrichment Foundation helps people learn, then earn, a living.

It's working. Self-starters like Lee Champion who hatched business ideas in the York Business Opportunity Centre incubator have created almost three hundred full- and part-time jobs during the past decade. Thousands more people have either found work or started businesses after getting help under the Learning Enrichment Foundation roof. A report from the Organization for Economic Co-operation and Development called the foundation a model for training and partnership with business.

"Something greater than our individual programs is created from all of us working together," says the director of the Centre, Pam Richardson. "You can train until you're blue in the face, but unless it's combined with whatever other needs a person may have, such as day-care, it won't be as successful as it could be."

Towards an Economy Based on Values

These accounts are three snapshots, three glimpses into the rebirth taking place in Canada's economic life. This is not the so-called "new economy" trumpeted by Canada's economic and political elite, one marked by tragically high levels of unemployment, anxiety and a growing gap between rich and poor, an economy which leaves many people on the sidelines.

It's a rebirth of hope, based on the realization that the mainstream economy fails to meet the needs of huge numbers of Canadians. We have all been touched, in some way, by the failure of that mainstream economy as it reels under the impact of technological change, corporate and government down-sizing, and free trade. It leaves its mark by our own unemployment or

15

under-employment, or that of someone close to us; by the frustration and cynicism of young people we know, unable to crack the job market at all or else dead-ended in boring, low-paying jobs; by the anxiety in those we know who still have jobs, but worry whether they'll last. For millions of Canadians, the "jobless recovery" is no abstraction; it is all too painfully human.

In response, a growing number of local citizens, social service agencies, First Nations, community groups, churches, budding entrepreneurs and others are launching their own businesses and local economic development efforts. These various strands of economic self-help, taken together, have become known as community-based economic development—CED for short.

Communities all over Canada are worried about holding on to the jobs and industries they have, and about attracting new ones. The standard approach has been to attract outside investment through a variety of business-oriented incentives. Yet while most of Canada is increasingly locked into a corporate-dominated approach to the economy, the CED path to development is slowly taking root. It's built around basic human needs, especially the need to work, and a recognition that everyone has a contribution to make, including those so often left out of the mainstream economy.

Joan Kuyek, a community organizer and writer in Sudbury, Ontario, notes that corporate-oriented economic values have become so powerful as to have "religious" status in our society. Yet when we try to challenge the assumptions and workings of the mainstream economy, "we are told that we're not 'realistic' and don't understand good business practice," says Kuyek. "We need to reclaim and re-name economics for ourselves" ("Which side are we on?" *Community Economics,* Fall 1996, 11).

Canada's Catholic bishops emphasized the need to take a hard look at the failings of the mainstream economy and to consider new strategies in their prophetic statement, *Ethical Reflections on the Economic Crisis,* issued in 1982. The statement—dismissed as unrealistic by the mainstream media and business leaders—noted that the recession of the early 1980s was ravaging the lives of many Canadians. "People must have a chance to choose their economic future rather than have one forced upon them," wrote the bishops. "The present economic crisis . . . reveals a deepening moral disorder in the values and priorities of our society" (*Canadian Churches and Social Justice,* edited by John R. Williams, Toronto: Anglican Book Centre and James Lorimer and Co., 1984, 96).

Reminding the church, and society overall, of the moral underpinnings of our economy is a challenge which the church continues to put before Canadians. "The gospel calls us, as people of faith, to voice our concerns about the serious failures in social responsibility we see around us," Canadian church leaders reminded us in their 1997 statement, *Restless for the Reign of God.* "We believe that all economic choices are ultimately moral choices."

That yearning for an economy based on values, one which demystifies the world of economics and returns it to manageable human proportions, helps explain the recent surge of interest in community economic development. CED is about returning to the original concept of economics, which means managing the household. It reflects hands-on efforts by people to choose their economic future.

That emphasis on values can be seen in my favourite definition of community economic development (and there are many): CED is like a potluck supper to which everybody brings something to share, and from which nobody goes away hungry.

"We've allowed economics to be analyzed not as a political question, but as a set of mathematical concepts divorced from politics," observes Greg Ramm, director of the Institute for Community Economics in Cambridge, Massachusetts. "That's extremely dangerous. Economics is a moral and ethical science—how you and I relate to each other, how we place value on each other, how we relate to the natural world."

Community economic development is a response to dramatic changes in our social and economic life. It isa community movement responding to the loss of work and the destruction of entire communities. The changes affecting our economy are so pervasive that every region of Canada has been affected. CED is an effort to develop economic strategies at the local level, instead of leaving economic decision-making in the hands of forces largely controlled from outside the community, if not from outside the country.

Four Fundamental Beliefs

CED grows out of four fundamental beliefs. One is that social and economic goals can and should be combined. That is, it's possible to develop businesses which are successful and which try to meet unmet needs in society, such as environmental protection or jobs for the unemployed. An outstanding example is the Edmonton Recycling Society, which was formed in 1988 to provide jobs for physically or mentally disadvantaged people. Since then, it has trained over five hundred people and now provides seventy full-time jobs, a quarter of them to people who had been on social assistance. By combining that social goal with hard-nosed business skills, including excellent marketing, it has developed into a profitable business. It operates without government grants and has returned more than $800,000 to the City of Edmonton through operating surpluses as it recycles more than half of Edmonton's garbage. John Bird tells the tale of the ERS in Chapter 5.

The second fundamental belief is that "business as usual" just isn't good enough. Or, as Greg MacLeod, a Catholic priest and spark-plug behind a range of community business ventures in Cape Breton, says, "The conventional capitalist system is not working." In particular, CED grows out of a realization that the mainstream economy, even an expanding mainstream economy, still leaves many people on the sidelines, relegated to unemployment, poverty and frustration. As long-time CED consultant and organizer Stewart Perry says, "By itself, business development cannot create the number and kind of jobs people need to get out of their marginalized status."

"CED is, more than anything else, a response to the failure of our advanced capitalist system to meet the basic needs of an increasingly large part of the population through the market," writes social-work teacher and community activist Eric Shragge, author of *Community Economic Development: In Search of Empowerment.* "The market has not only produced extended periods of unemployment, precarious low-wage jobs, and total exclusion for many from the labour market, but as a consequence, has marginalized a large population politically and socially" (Black Rose Books, 1993, 7).

The third major conviction behind CED is the recognition of the human need to work, and that good living and good working go together. Its reaffirmation of what Catholic social teaching calls "the priority of labour" stands in sharp contrast to the "jobless future" offered by the corporate economy. Work is not just a source of income, but a central element of what it means to be fully human. It enables people to relate to others, and to exercise their creativity. Without work, people lack pride and dignity, and much more. As theologian Matthew Fox observes, "When work is denied a people, hope is the first casualty" (*The Reinvention of Work,* San Francisco: Harper, 1995, 10).

The fourth foundational element is the "C" in CED: community. Most Canadian strategies to alleviate poverty or to sponsor economic growth have focussed on individuals, through such programs as skills training or support for individual entrepreneurs by means of grants and loans. In contrast, CED is based on and affirms the role of the community. That community can be a community of interest, such as psychiatric patients, youth or aboriginal people. It can be a geographic community, such as a particular neighbourhood, city or region. Or it can be a community made up of different kinds of people, linked by a willingness to work together for the common good, through such means as a credit union or a community development corporation.

Many community-based economic initiatives are small and in the start-up phase. Some, however, are more substantial and work in a range of areas to nurture local economic development. The Community Business Resource Centre in Toronto, for example, works with four thousand people each year, many of them new Canadians, providing the training needed to survive in today's tough economic climate. Eighty percent of those who participate in

19

entrepreneurship training go on to start their own businesses. The centre has also helped six community and co-op businesses get started, has co-sponsored Ontario-wide CED conferences, and sponsors three community loan funds for people unable to obtain funding from conventional sources.

Here are some other examples of this grassroots economic revival:

◆ In Cape Breton, a hundred people are working at a rope company, an inn, a plumbing company and other businesses, through New Dawn Enterprises, a community-owned development corporation, and through a venture capital company with strong community links called BCA Holdings. John Bird takes an in-depth look at New Dawn in Chapter 4.

◆ The Human Resource Development Association (HRDA) of Halifax was set up twenty years ago to help people move from welfare to work in a humane way. Today HRDA continues to achieve that goal by developing viable businesses, along with employee training and support services. Its businesses employ a hundred and fifty people.

◆ Hundreds of women living on farms and in small towns throughout southern and eastern Ontario are launching their own businesses, and supporting each other, through a grassroots movement called Women and Rural Economic Development.

◆ About forty self-described "survivors" of the mental health system are working in a supportive environment for A-Way Express, a Toronto courier company set up to provide jobs for people who have a particularly difficult time finding work.

◆ As money gets tight, people are turning to barter systems such as the Local Employment and Trading System (LETS), through which they exchange goods and services with each other using "green dollars." As a result, people with little or no cash can obtain what they need, and use their skills to do so, rather than relying on charity.

As these examples show, community economic development can take many forms: community development corporations, worker co-operatives, self-employment support services, barter networks. (Community development corporations are non-profit corporations set up to strengthen the economic and social development of local communities.)

Canada's aboriginal people are increasingly involved in starting their own businesses. Various businesses launched by the Kitsaki Development Corporation in northern Saskatchewan are among the most notable successes in aboriginal CED. Begun to counter an eighty-five percent unemployment rate among members of the La Ronge Indian Band, Kitsaki's ventures include a hotel, wild rice growing, a meat company, trucking and other businesses, many of them joint ventures with private firms. These businesses now employ about two hundred people full-time.

Some governments at various levels have helped nurture local economic action. Under Saskatchewan's now-defunct Community Bonds program, the province guaranteed the capital of people investing in local business ventures. That unleashed some remarkable examples of community power. In the town of Rosetown, where people were worried about young people leaving because of a lack of jobs, six hundred people invested an average of $1,300 in community bonds to lure Precision Metal Fabricating Ltd. to town. It worked. The thirty-five jobs provided by Precision are significant in a town of only 2,800 people.

Ontario's former NDP Government actively promoted CED through a range of measures, including Jobs Ontario Community Action grants and support for community organizations, a CED Secretariat and legislation establishing community loan funds. Those initiatives helped raise awareness about community economic development and provided valuable funding, although these measures have all been abolished by Ontario's current Conservative regime.

Another major government CED initiative is the federally funded Community Futures Program, which works to promote community development through broadly-based community strategic planning. In the southern Ontario town of Port Colborne, for instance, 450 people took part in a community economic planning

21

process, which has led to a new marina, business workshops, an Opportunity-Career Centre, a tourism co-ordinator and other new initiatives.

The Community Futures Program has made it possible to raise the money needed for local business development, through Community Futures Development Corporations. These corporations are eligible for base investment portfolios of $1.5 million, funded by the federal government to help create permanent jobs in local communities. Each centre is governed by a volunteer board drawn from local business people. In Ontario alone, these corporations have provided 9,600 loans worth $230.7 million since 1986. These loans have helped create or maintain over forty-six thousand jobs.

The common thread which unites the various community economic development efforts is that they all involve local citizens, organizations and other partners taking action at the community level to create jobs and strengthen local communities. CED, then, stands out from the traditional model of economic development, which relies on private investors, often from outside a community, to start businesses. Instead, it's a strategy which taps both the human and financial resources found in local communities.

By enabling people to work together, community economic development holds out the promise of a qualitatively different, more human-scale economy and society overall. Many CED enterprises combine business development with environmental concerns, democratic decision-making and inclusion of hard-to-employ people.

A Movement Reborn

Community economic development is not new, although the term itself is fairly new. One need only think of the Antigonish Movement for local economic self-reliance which flourished in rural Nova Scotia during the 1930s. Led by Jimmy Tompkins and Moses Coady, two Catholic priests, the Antigonish Movement promoted co-operatives as a way to lift people up out of poverty.

The Movement sparked the formation of co-operative stores, fishing co-ops and regional organizations like the United Maritime

Fishermen. Credit unions were formed, which gave low-income people access to credit for the first time.

The rise of credit unions, especially in Quebec, and the wheat pools on the prairies are other examples of the large-scale movements by Canadians to regain control over their economic lives. Taken together, these efforts amount to a strong "social economy" made up of co-operatively owned businesses, credit unions, consumer co-operatives, non-profit day-care centres, and other not-for-profit enterprises.

This social economy has had a considerable impact—much more than many Canadians realize. Twelve million Canadians belong to at least one co-operative. As businesses and other enterprises formed by people pooling their resources to obtain the goods and services they need, co-ops represent an important effort to regain local economic control. These co-ops span a huge variety of activities, including financial services (credit unions and *caisses populaires*), fishing, forestry, food distribution, funerals, day-care, and much more. Canada's two-thousand-plus housing co-ops are home to about 250,000 people.

Co-operatives provide an effective way for communities of people to bring control of the economy back into their own hands. Democratic control, based on the principle of one person, one vote, is perhaps the most important co-op value.

In certain areas the social economy is very significant, providing a real alternative to the mainstream, corporate-dominated economy. The co-ops of Evangeline in P.E.I. have already been mentioned. In the small town of Cheticamp, Nova Scotia, ten co-ops provide about three hundred jobs, including the fish plant, a retail store, the credit union, a seniors' housing co-op, a youth employment co-op, and others.

While Canadians have launched community-inspired economic action such as co-operatives for decades, what is new today is the sharp rise of interest in community economic development. The continuing crisis of unemployment, coupled with government cutbacks to social services, is prompting a search for new solutions to the needs of low-income people. A wide range of community organizations, social service agencies, local business associations, governments, churches, and other groups have been actively interested in, and involved in, CED. More and more it is seen as a new strategy with the potential to crack the poverty-welfare cycle in which so many Canadians are trapped. Several hundred CED businesses and organizations are active in Ontario alone; across Canada, the number would total several thousand. Community economic development is increasingly on the public agenda, through conferences, forums and networks.

Community economic development is getting talked about, and acted upon, far more than it was ten or twenty years ago. It is working its way increasingly into discussions and proposals for a more humane and moral economy. The Alternative Federal Budget advocated by the Canadian Centre for Policy Alternatives and Choices, a Winnipeg-based social justice group, includes CED as part of its strategy for a more democratic economy. The movement has spawned a national newsletter, *Making Waves*. The popularity of CED perhaps can be seen in the fact that the Conference Board of Canada has established a Business in the Community Forum to encourage corporate involvement in CED.

"Community economic development has come of age," says David Pell, executive director of the Community Business Resource Centre in Toronto and someone who has worked in CED across Canada for twenty years. "The growth has been significant, both in terms of numbers of businesses and the number of people involved." Another change, notes Pell, is that community business organizers are more sophisticated in terms of the skills and knowledge needed to be successful.

"After twenty-five years in the trenches, working to build community economies, I can still be inspired by the creativity, dedication and results being achieved by people and organizations that refuse to be hypnotized by the mantra of globalization," says Mike Lewis, one of Canada's leading authorities on CED and contributor to *Reinventing the Local Economy* (Stewart E. Perry, Vernon, B.C.: Centre for Community Enterprise, 1994).

Band-Aid or Breakthrough?

So far, so good, but is community economic development a real alternative? That is, does it have the capacity really to make a dent in Canada's unemployment crisis, to provide decent, well-paying jobs, and to hold out at least some prospect for a more humane, people-centred economy?

These are difficult questions. Before answering them, we need to look at the position of the CED movement in relation to the broader economy. Canada is very much part of an economy dominated by global corporations, marked by capital mobility and rapid technological change. Governments at all levels are cutting back on their direct influence in the economy, paving the way for even greater corporate dominance. The results mean an economy marked by increasing polarization of wealth and opportunity, and one in which private business is by far the most powerful economic player.

Where does that leave community business efforts? In and of themselves, they are not a substitute for the failings of the mainstream economy and of the persistently high levels of unemployment and poverty resulting from that economy. Many CED businesses involve people on the margins of the economy working in organizations which themselves are poorly-funded and have had, at best, mixed success. Speaking of women's businesses, for example, Cathy Lang of the Canadian Co-operative Association asks: "How many women's groups have developed businesses in catering, cleaning, crafts or sewing? Is poorly paid 'women's work' the way to encourage women to enter the formal economy? CED initiatives must not be seen as a cure-all to 'correct' the consequences of repressive economic policies." Joan Kuyek voices similar concerns, noting how many small businesses begun by women are only marginally successful due to inadequate resources and a depressed economic climate.

Eric Shragge of Montreal is one of a growing number of people who believe that community economic development must be linked to an agenda for broader economic and political change. "We have to see the limits of CED," says Shragge. "We're dealing with catastrophic levels of unemployment. Small business developments employing six or eight people can't make up for a local factory which shuts down and throws four hundred people out of work. There's a danger in the CED model of separating local activity from broader issues of ownership, wealth and power."

In his book, *Community Economic Development: In Search of Empowerment*, Shragge writes that "CED must be a force for social change that challenges the current situations of unemployment and precarious employment. The challenges that CED can bring are the creation of a new type of economic development that does not put profit, growth, and environmental destruction over social and other needs, but sees itself as an alternative to the private market while using it" (Black Rose, 1997, ix).

Similarly, John Restakis, former CED project manager for the Canadian Co-operative Association, asks, "How does CED create long-term, high-wage jobs? How does it address the problem of access to capital? What is its role in job training? . . . . It is not enough to say that community economic development is a formula for empowering the victims and outcasts of our economic system. To be meaningful, it must address the economic structures that create victims and outcasts in the first place" ("From Margins to Mainstream: Developing a Strategic Vision for CED," *Community Economics,* Fall 1995, 6).

This means that community economic development can't be seen in isolation. Rather, it's part of a broader movement for economic justice, one which embodies biblical values of justice and stewardship, and one which enables some of the people excluded from the mainstream economy to regain dignity in their lives and some control over their livelihoods.

Despite the challenges that it faces, and the fact that CED by itself cannot remedy an unjust economy, the track record of community economic action has shown that it can make a difference. At a time when our destinies seem to be under the sway of the global economy and its powerful masters, this record is both a cause of hope and a challenge to progressive people to strengthen local economic initiatives and to ensure that CED becomes linked to the broader movement for social justice.

Responding in Faith

The issues raised by the failings of our economic system are spiritual and moral ones. Unemployment and the poverty, isolation and frustration which scar the lives of hundreds of thousands of Canadians call for what the Bible calls *metanoia*, a change of heart. With its deep spiritual heritage, the church could play a leading role in encouraging a radical re-thinking about how we organize our economy. "The church has a profound moral and ethical contribution to make to the discussion about our economic, political and social future. In a world that seems to devalue human life, the church calls for the sanctity of life and the necessity to live life in community" (*Sustainable Social Economics, A Proposed Social Statement of the Evangelical Lutheran Church in Canada,* 1996, 27). Kevin Arsenault delves into the links between community economic development and Christian faith in the next chapter.

Churches and church members across Canada are heavily involved in meeting the basic needs of people hardest hit by cuts in social programs and chronic unemployment, the front-line victims of what former United Church Moderator Marion Best aptly calls "the war against the poor." That ministry is essential. Yet in itself, it's not enough. The church needs to raise broader issues of economic justice and use its resources to plant seeds which can grow into an economy reflecting gospel values.

The fact that community economic development is attracting broader interest and support within the churches is itself a sign of hope. The 1997 statement by church leaders cited earlier, *Restless for the Reign of God,* mentions CED among the signposts of the reign of God. It presents community-shared agriculture programs, worker co-ops, barter systems and community loan funds as examples of these signposts.

Yet statements must be backed up by action. Our wish—the dream that inspired this book—is that, by learning of these examples of faith-based local economic development, you and other readers of this book will be inspired to become advocates and organizers of community economic development where you live. We also hope to deepen and broaden the debate about how the church can respond to the economic crisis and can remind people of faith that there *are* alternatives. The Canada that we hand down to our children does not need to be a continuation of what we have now.

The examples of community economic development in the following pages have been selected to spread Good News in these dark times, to show how committed Christians are making a difference in their communities. Their efforts help counter the "economic fatalism" so common in Canada today.

CHAPTER 3

Babylon Revisited: CED and the Economic Injustice of Our Times

KEVIN ARSENAULT

What kind of economy is God calling us to build? This chapter explores the heart of the issue from a faith perspective: our current corporate-dominated economy, the call of the gospel, and the promise of CED. Taking our faith seriously means taking a hard look at the principalities and powers in our midst, and refusing to give in to what has been aptly termed the "TINA syndrome"—There Is No Alternative (to the status quo).

When we think about the sense of powerlessness that so many people feel today, the growing gap between rich and poor, and the concentration of wealth and power in the hands of a powerful elite, we see that the economic crisis grows out of a spiritual crisis. We see this more clearly through a comparison between our times and Babylonian times.

Community economic development provides a way to live out the central commandment to love your neighbour as yourself.

There is an intrinsic link between living an authentic life of Christian discipleship and the kinds of personal and social practices associated with community economic development. Both share a common objective: the establishment of a more just and humane community through moral action.

We sense this connection in the following chapters when we hear how Christians have committed themselves to building a better world through democratic economic organization, courageous action and hard work. It is this link between values and alternative outcomes that makes their stories so compelling. It shows us—notwithstanding the difficulties—how the values and vision of Christianity can inspire people to live dignified and ethical lives in accordance with their faith. We see God at work in the transformation of our world through these community business initiatives.

Embarking on a serious reflection on the connection between CED and Christian faith can be threatening, however. Thinking too long about what is possible may lead us to places we may not want to go. It may demand that we change the way we are living, and make sacrifices and commitments to God. That's when our fear that we are not equal to the call can lead us to co-operate with evil institutions that destroy life and hurt millions of people.

Given the all-encompassing character of transnational corporate empires in today's world, it is not moral to accept the idea of "living in the empire." To do so is to contribute to the poverty and exploitation which those empires perpetuate throughout the world. Instead, we must seek to transform the empire by reflecting the love of God in courageous acts of peaceful and creative defiance. We need to recall the words of St. Paul, who wrote to Christians living in the capital city of the Roman empire: "Do not be conformed to this world but be transformed by the renewal of your mind" (Romans 12:2). God is always at work in the world. We are called to detect the workings of God's Spirit in new social formations that encourage peace and justice, and to support social organizations that strive to build moral community.

There is no shortage of models, ideas and groups available for those who realize that our efforts to advance the reign of God must extend to our economic life. We can become involved in solidarity movements or join intentional communities and co-operatives. We can take our investments out of banks and put them into local credit unions and venture capital funds that stimulate local businesses.

With the rapid advance of the new world era in which transnational corporate empires rule the world, these examples of CED become truly prophetic. They offer inspirational and practical models of social organization, helping us combat despair. They urge us to evaluate what God would prefer us to do if we had a choice about how the world should be structured and about our role in that process. They provide occasions for the conversion of moral consciousness. The key question becomes: "Do we believe we have a choice?"

Ethical Reflections on Building a Moral Economy

We are witnessing massive social and personal change. Look at our hectic routines and increased stresses, not to mention the changing patterns in the ways we relate to one another. Everything seems in flux: the economic security we had on Tuesday is downsized away on Wednesday. No warning. No apology.

People feel adrift in this sea of change. We may not understand all the details, but we know very well that a few benefit from the way things are, while many of us lose. And we sense that we are being changed by powerful ideas and forces that are global in nature, but affect our local communities.

We lament many of the changes imposed in our workplaces, schools and hospitals. In fact, we wouldn't wish them on our worst enemy. Yet we feel compelled to comply with them because they are imposed from somewhere far beyond our communities, by who knows whom. Changes come suddenly as announcements in the news, "done deals" that cannot be undone. We need to survive and carry on with our lives, so we accept them. Yet gradual changes bring a much more complete transformation over time. Slowly but surely we begin to accept lower moral standards. We justify our actions or simply turn our attention away from areas of tension or conflict and numb our awareness. We start to live in a state of minimal consciousness, avoiding the thought of our compliance with an immoral system. We see ourselves as powerless, without an option, caught in a culture and economy that rob life of dignity and hope. We believe there is nowhere else to go. That's the message our dominant culture keeps preaching. This is a culture shaped by social institutions like the mass media which are largely owned by transnational corporations and primarily interested in exploiting people through consumer-oriented advertising. We are afraid to challenge these forces: they are too obscure and too powerful.

Yet if we wish truly to understand and evaluate the moral nature of the present age, we have no choice but to learn how we cooperate in social sin, and how we are entangled in a complex, immoral system of global economics. We can do this if we strive to see the world with the same moral clarity with which we recognize the social sins of previous ages, such as the Spanish Inquisition, the enslavement of millions of people of different race and colour, or the shameless murder of millions in the Holocaust.

Tracing the steps in the ladder of influence leading from the local level to the hegemony of transnational corporations is a monumental task. It goes beyond the scope of this chapter. I want, however, to do four things: examine the rise of transnational empires; look at how transnational corporate control has changed our consciousness; consider the idolatry of this global economic system from a biblical perspective; and finally, explore a foundational theology to transform these deadly economies in practical ways.

The Twenty-First Century
—Era of Transnational Empires

A massive power shift has been underway in the world for some time. We are aware that economic and political power is being transferred from nation states to transnational corporations, from public control to private control. News reports remind us that life for many is getting harsher, while corporate profits are soaring. More people are falling into poverty, while global elites grow more powerful and wealthy. Transnational corporations and international traders and financiers accumulate riches from peoples and places everywhere, in ways that inflict death on the earth through pollution, deforestation, monocultural farming and mining.

This shift has not been accidental. Governments have transferred power to corporations through policies designed to diminish or eliminate regulation of the private sector. Free-trade agreements have weakened democratic power by granting new rights to corporations. As a result, international trade and global financial processes are being directed by powerful men in corporate boardrooms, not by political leaders in legislative assemblies. Legislative efforts by democratically elected governments to effect social change on behalf of people or the environment are diminishing throughout the world.

As we usher in the next millennium, we enter a new era of global corporate rule by transnationals. A fundamental theology for today's world must take this situation into account. To avoid the assimilating and corrupting impact of their influence in our lives, we must understand the nature of transnational empires. We need to judge them against the values and principles of our Christian faith. We then need to discover practical ways to resist and free ourselves from captivity in the empire. I believe that community economic development can be a key element in that resistance.

The first step is to understand the power of the transnational corporations. They undermine the political power of countries to regulate market activity and protect human beings and environmental standards. They do this by operating internationally, beyond the control of regulations and national laws, using sophisticated telecommunications technology.

To put this power into perspective, consider a few statistics taken from a 1996 report of the Institute for Policy Analysis in Washington, D.C., *The Top 200: The Rise of Global Corporate Power* (Sarah Anderson and John Cavanagh, Washington, D.C.: Institute for Policy Analysis). There are 191 countries in the world. Wal-Mart's total sales world-wide for 1995 were greater than the economies of 161 of those 191 countries. Think about it: only 30 countries in the world have economies bigger than Wal-Mart's! American tobacco giant Philip Morris operates in more than 170 countries and has more economic clout than New Zealand. Of the 100 largest economies in the world, 51 are now global corporations; only 49 are countries. The top 200 corporations control well over a quarter of the world's economic activity. These mega-money-making systems do not share their wealth with their workers. Further, they leave the remainder of the world's workers in poverty: of the approximately 2.6 billion workers in the world (slightly less than half the total world population of 5.6 billion), the top 200 global corporations employ only 18.8 million people. That's less than one-hundredth of one percent of the world's workers!

The global emperors ruling the private market have free rein to implement their business plans without interference from elected governments. On May 8, 1997, three appointed judges of the World Trade Organization issued a decision: from now on, nations will no longer have the right to develop their own health and safety standards if these are more restrictive than those crafted by un-elected and unaccountable international bodies (*Toronto Star*, May 10, 1997). Indeed, governments act as willing accomplices in the corporate agenda of privatization. They no longer seem willing to regulate and tax adequately transnationals and their international economic activity. National governments throughout the world are rushing to eliminate public institutions in local communities. They are selling public utilities and community-based services such as health and education to corporations, even when these services generate significant revenues for government.

The long-standing ethic of co-operation which has been a defining characteristic of Canadian society is being rapidly displaced by the privatization of the economy, globalism and the ethic of "might is right."

From Global Village to Global Pillage
—From Optimism to Despair

Let's get to the heart of the matter. How does the dominant ideology of our society affect how people think and feel?

When people are plunged into a life of fear and misery by economic systems that deny them freedom and dignity, their capacity for creative development is diminished. Suffering perpetuates despair, violence and unhappiness. More and more people who are excluded from participation in society know this. Feelings of anxiety and despair pervade because things are indeed bleaker, but they are worsened by the illegitimate claims of today's dominant cultural ideology.

Our actions are shaped by the opportunities and limits we encounter in our social situation. Our attitudes and values are also shaped by the presentation of ideas and images through the media and other social institutions. The media, controlled by transnational corporations, tell us that the privileges our system affords transnational corporations must be respected. Little is said about corporate obligations to society or the environment. Accordingly, transnational empires direct social change through an international economic system that reaches into the day-to-day lives and consciousness of people, while democracy drowns in the rising tide of corporate power.

More and more people are realizing the true nature of the "New World Order," the vision of a "global village" promoted just a few years ago as the next great era of human unity and prosperity. In place of a global village, we are witnessing global pillage. All of this has affected how we feel. If we shift our focus from the hard facts which define our modern situation and ask ourselves what we are thinking and feeling, we detect a categorical shift in our collective state of consciousness. Many people are depressed, pessimistic, and struggling to find meaning in their lives, purpose in their work, and hope for tomorrow. Many fear the future. Others are simply exhausted by it all. The emotional consequence of this state of consciousness and life experience can be extremely disabling. It can stifle the spirit and compromise the moral integrity of our lives.

The radical "emotional" shift which has affected our consciousness results from the cultural shift in dominant ideology during the past ten to fifteen years. It has left us largely unprepared to challenge the situation we now face. It has neutralized the courage and confidence that come from a dynamic, living faith. Dashed hopes lead to dashed lives. Despair is becoming our greatest temptation. It can easily lead to compliance with evil, because the consequences of despair are often depression and lethargy, two key ingredients for conformity with an immoral social system.

Unlike the external shift in society—from political to economic rulers—the change in human consciousness represents a completely different phase. The cultural shift experienced at the level of human consciousness is not simply a benign consequence of liberal ideology, but a symptom of its death. With its demise we are offered a closed neo-liberal future driven by a ruthless economic ethic of competition. In the wake of the transnational empires, it is all too easy to fall into the trap of believing that the death of our most cherished aspirations signals the death of human freedom.

Dominant ideologies seek to hide the truth, to distort or disguise insightful social information. Distorted information about the availability of future options aggravates our mood of psychological and political powerlessness. The trickle-down theory of economics offered short-term benefits to keep alive the neo-liberal promise that things would get better. Those benefits have now dried up and the promises of neo-liberalism have been exposed as illusions. These illusions hid the deeper truths about our society, blinding us to the warnings from prophets that our capitalist society would eventually become a world of insupportable gaps between wealthy global elites and the masses of the world's poor. Many people now fear the future, no longer believing the neo-liberal dreams they were taught.

The dominant "ideology of inevitability" enlists people as pawns in a global neo-liberal economic project. This is economic tyranny and social determinism wrapped up in one, a crafty disguise to mask the impact transnational corporations have on the suffering in the world. "The cult of inevitability," the world view that has no optimism for the future, that accepts global injustice as a necessary evil, would have a crippling effect upon us. It presents a future in which we accept what is offered in order to survive, not a future fashioned from our best moral and spiritual aspirations to build a just and sustainable world.

If we can no longer hope in the promises of our neo-liberal economic culture, must we accept that the future is fixed? Christians find their inspiration and hope in the promises of God, not in the promises of neo-liberalism. Our faith demands that we challenge the dominant ideology of our day. It is critical to understand the difference between neo-liberal optimism and Christian hope. We are optimistic when we believe that the things we strive for in this world can be attained; we are hopeful when we respond to God's call to do the right thing, even in the face of evidence that the good things we strive for may not be attained, at least not in our lifetimes.

No matter how we define neo-liberalism as an economic system, from the perspective of Christian principles and values, in principle it is immoral. It excludes huge numbers of people from meaningful participation in society and a fair share of the world's wealth. The top 200 global corporations have almost twice the economic clout of four-fifths of the world's population. According to the United Nations, eighty-five percent of the world's economy is controlled by one-fifth of humanity; only fifteen percent is controlled by the poorest four-fifths, 4.5 billion people.

Canada's Catholic bishops have challenged the moral legitimacy of the neo-liberal system of global economics in a recent statement: "The current catastrophic state of the world eloquently shows what happens when neo-liberal economic policies impoverish women and men. Instead, economic democratization, genuine redistributive reforms and the resulting strengthening of civil society should be the primary goals" (*The Struggle against Poverty: A Sign of Hope for Our World*, Pastoral Letter, 1996).

If we reflect on biblical concepts of past empires which dominated the people of God, we can see how the belief that "there is no alternative" can lead to moral indifference and assimilation into the values and practices of an idolatrous economic system.

Is Biblical Babylon a Mirror for Our Times?

Some Christian fundamentalists try to interpret references in prophetic and apocalyptic biblical texts as literal references to present-day places and world events. Yet Jesus dissuaded his disciples from wanting to know the details of the last days. He taught them that what really mattered was for them to remain faithful to his teachings. Biblical accounts of Babylon nonetheless offer images and understandings that mirror our age. They provide insights into the nature of transnational empires, help us understand why we feel compelled to submit to them, and point to what we need in order to combat this deceptive, debilitating attack on our faith in God. Although our world may not look much like the world of biblical times, the empires of old bear an uncanny resemblance to today's empires. The two key similarities are the domination of other nations through finance and trade on a transnational scale; and the seduction of political rulers and the assimilation of most people into the empire's dominant culture, which encourages selfishness, individualism and various forms of idolatry.

In the Old Testament book of Jeremiah, Babylon is said to rule over "all the kingdoms of the world which are on the face of the earth" (Jer. 25:26; 27:7). It is portrayed as a wealthy and unjust transnational economic system, not simply a city or region of the world: "O you [Babylon] who dwell by many waters, rich in treasures, your end has come, the thread of your life is cut" (Jer. 51:13). The domination of the Babylonian empire was total enough to earn it the title "destroyer of nations" (Jer. 4:7). In the New Testament book of Revelation, the image of Babylon is also that of "the great city which has dominion over the kings of the earth" (Rev. 17:18), which "is seated upon many waters"

(Rev. 17:1). The waters are said to be "peoples and crowds, and nations and tongues" (Rev. 17:15).

How did Babylon gain control over other nations? Jeremiah suggests at least a degree of wilful participation on the part of nations: "The nations drank of her [Babylon's] wine, therefore the nations went mad" (Jer. 51:6). What was this wine? It seems that under Babylonian rule the peoples of other nations were gradually transformed from a people who worshipped God into a people who worshipped false gods. Babylon not only captured bodies, it also corrupted souls, enticing people to abandon their faith for participation in the dominant culture and a competitive economic system: "For from the least to the greatest of them, every one is greedy for unjust gain . . ." (Jer. 6:13).

The faith of the people in Jeremiah's day waned not simply because false prophets deceived them, but because the people deceived themselves: "The prophets prophesy falsely, and the priests rule at their direction; my people love to have it so . . ." (Jer. 5:31; see also 14:14). Why did the people prefer to believe falsehoods? Perhaps they had lost hope in the possibility of a political alternative to Babylonian rule and sought to become comfortable with the type of privatized life Babylon had to offer: "But they say, 'That is in vain! We will follow our own plans, and will every one act according to the stubbornness of his evil heart'"(Jer. 18:8; see also Jer. 2:25). We are told that they so deceived themselves that they believed their practice of idolatry was actually sustaining them (Jer. 44:17).

As in the writings of Jeremiah, Revelation tells how the nations were not simply captured by Babylon, but were seduced to forfeiting their power to an international system of trade and commerce: "For thy [Babylon's] merchants were the great men of the earth, and all nations were deceived by thy sorcery" (Rev. 18:23).

Jeremiah obviously regarded such a social situation as unsustainable. His prophecy was that Babylon's domination over the economy and resources of other nations would eventually come to an abrupt end: "The nations shall no longer flow to him [the king of Babylon]; the wall of Babylon has fallen" (Jer. 51:44). Who are the people saddened by the collapse of the transnational system called Babylon? Those who profited from social injustice.

According to Revelation, it is "the merchants of the earth [who] have grown rich with the wealth of her [Babylon's] wantonness" (Rev 18: 3). Along with the political leaders who forfeited their power (and peoples) to her, they lament her collapse, and the collapse of the international trading system: "And the kings of the earth . . . will weep and wail over her . . ." (Rev. 18:9). "And the merchants of the earth weep and mourn for her, since no one buys their cargo any more" (Rev. 18:9-11). "And they threw dust on their heads, as they wept and mourned, crying out, 'Alas, alas, for the great city where all who had ships at sea grew rich by her wealth! In one hour she has been laid waste'" (Rev. 18:19).

Jeremiah delivered an unmistakably clear prophetic message to God's people about how they should relate to Babylon: "Flee from the midst of Babylon" (Jer 51:6; 51:45). The New Testament presents a similar prophetic message to those living in Babylon just prior to the collapse of this international system: "Then I heard another voice from heaven saying, 'Come out of her [Babylon], my people, lest you take part in her sins, lest you share in her plagues; for her sins are heaped high as heaven, and God has remembered her iniquities'" (Rev. 18:4).

Nearly all nations today have allowed a global economic system of wealth and power to shape their domestic social and economic policies. Laws and trade agreements clearly benefit corporations. The owners of transnational corporations have become wealthy by exploiting people and the earth's resources. Cooperating with such a system corrupts the moral fabric of our lives as Christians. Believing that we have no choice but to acquiesce leads to a mind-numbing state of denial and despair as we settle for mere survival in the empire.

In a speech to former heads of state and government in 1996, Prime Minister Jean Chrétien acknowledged that Canada's dependence on international finance is eroding our ability to "control our economic destiny," creating a volatile situation where "a nation-state can seem powerless." Rather than challenging this situation and outlining an alternative course for Canada's future, however, the Prime Minister said "we cannot stop globalization," and we must "adjust to it" (Address to the 14th Plenary of the InterAction Council of Former Heads of State and Government, Vancouver, B.C., May 19, 1996). The problem is not merely a technical, economic problem: the roots of the disorder in society are ethical and spiritual.

In *Accountable All Together: Ways to Fight the Crisis,* Quebec's Catholic bishops noted that our economic crisis is really a spiritual crisis: "This crisis is not the result of fate or natural disaster. It can largely be explained by the perverted effects of an economy based on the pursuit of profit, excessive consumerism and the requirements of a free market. It is also the result of spiritual flaws that have weakened the moral framework of our community" (cited in *Catholic New Times,* May 4, 1997, 6).

Finding Hope Through Community

A theology of community economic development begins with reflection on the intrinsic link between the values of our faith and the experiences of community economic projects. We must weigh these CED efforts against the social and economic circumstances of today's world. That some churches, ministers and believers are nurturing economic development projects in their communities gives us hope in the midst of despair. They offer models that challenge the entire Christian church to follow their example.

As the organization Ten Days for Global Justice proclaimed in *Profits or Prophets?* (1997), "Finding alternatives to the way the world is must include an equal commitment to discovering new expressions of God at work in the world." We seek a world based on Jesus' vision of the reign of God. We contribute to such a world when we heed God's call to do justice. In an age in which money is worshipped, and winning out over others is the only practice rewarded by the dominant social system, doing justice requires a conscious return to the fundamentals of our faith, summed up in the two great commandments found in Scripture:

*"Teacher, which is the great commandment in the law?"
And he said to him, "You shall love the Lord your God
with all your heart, and with all your soul, and with all
your mind. This is the great and first commandment. And
a second is like it, You shall love your neighbour as
yourself."*

Matthew 22:36-39

Who is my neighbour? We decide who our neighbours will be by
our actions, not through abstract criteria. My neighbour is the person in need whom I can serve. The parable of the Good Samaritan
illustrates the simple, practical requirements of the love of God
and of neighbour. CED recognizes the priority of putting words
into action, of spiritual transformation through community actions
which aim to meet the needs of others. This is a core teaching of
our faith. Although we are healed and redeemed by the love of
God given freely, something we could not achieve on our own, we
only keep this precious gift intact by putting faith into action. As
St. James declares:

*What does it profit, my brethren, if a man says he has
faith but has not works? Can his faith save him? If a
brother or sister is ill-clad and in lack of daily food, and
one of you says to them, "Go in peace, be warmed and
filled," without giving them the things needed for the
body, what does it profit? So faith by itself, if it has no
works, is dead. But some one will say, "You have faith
and I have works." Show me your faith apart from your
works, and I by my works will show you my faith.*

James 2: 14-18

If we wish to be Good Samaritans today, we need first to meet our
neighbours and develop healthy relationships with them. We can
seek out the excluded, the forgotten, the homeless, all those who
live in the shadows of society close to our homes. This is what we
must do if we want to love God truly. As John tells us, there is no
other way we can be sure we are not deceiving ourselves when we
say we love God: "If any one says, 'I love God,' and hates his

brother [or sister], he is a liar; for he who does not love his brother [or sister] whom he has seen, cannot love God whom he has not seen" (1 John 4:20). Working to express our love for others through struggles with them to improve their situations is the paramount way we can show our love for God in an age that puts profits before people.

The goal of theological and ethical reflection is to discern God's will regarding the practical measures needed to establish moral human community. In an age of global economic injustice, we are called to replace destructive economic practices with sustainable human and social development. This requires action at the local level, action which fulfills Jesus' commandment: "A new commandment I give to you, that you love one another; even as I have loved you, that you also love one another" (John 13:34). It is the ethical opposite of the dominant ideology which says, "What is mine is mine, what is yours is yours." That some have billions while others starve may seem of no moral consequence to the dominant way of thinking today. Yet this situation is completely contrary to the gospel, and we cannot reconcile ourselves to it.

Faith and a commitment to the love of neighbour can strengthen our resistance to the dominant ethic of competition and social exclusion. Our resistance must be pro-active, working to build communities and practices that respect people and all life. Community economic development provides concrete ways of remaining faithful to these teachings and of resisting assimilation into a culture that glorifies self and virtually ignores the needs of other people.

The dominant culture is a powerful one, but it is not all of life. There are always counter-cultural and alternative expressions of culture within society that reflect our capacity to create something inspired by the Holy Spirit. God is truly at work in the world. It is up to us to discover God's presence and respond to the divine invitation to co-operate in transforming society and establishing the reign of God.

What is impossible for humankind is not impossible with God. With this in mind, we can discover reserves of courage, hope, faith and love. We can be inspired to imagine alternative ways to provide for our needs and the needs of others, ways which enhance our dignity. We can organize new ways of working and living that promote life rather than death. Above all, we can debunk the lie that there are no alternatives to "business as usual."

People working in community economic development recognize the need to challenge the dominant economic and social system. As the Canadian bishops put it in their pastoral letter on the elimination of poverty, *The Struggle Against Poverty: A Sign of Hope for Our World* (1996):

> Today, more than ever, Christians are called upon to follow in the footsteps of the prophets, in the footsteps of Jesus, by performing an extremely delicate, often controversial, but nonetheless essential service: denouncing social sin that oppresses and impoverishes their brothers and sisters. We remain convinced that the proper emphasis should be placed on the eradication of structural injustice, one sure cause of poverty. Personal conversion and true repentance through the promotion and practice of social change, inspired by the gospel, can further this goal.

The bishops identify how the dominant global system of economics is destroying the dignity and quality of life for millions of people. Christians involved in CED make life-choices that resist these destructive trends and practices. They look to one another to find alternative ways to meet their needs. By organizing and working together, they build relationships based on mutual concern and justice, and encourage social attitudes and practices that respect the rights and dignity of people. "Overcome evil with good" (Romans 12:21) is their motto, spoken or unspoken. Displacing the violence of the dominant economic system with the caring and compassion of a more co-operative one *is* possible.

The bottom line of community economic development is hope through resistance and a sense of our power together. Hope that a different, more moral society is possible is being kindled through local economic action. The emergence of community-based, environmentally sustainable businesses and projects to meet basic human needs demonstrates what we can accomplish together. Together they could grow into a movement strong enough to challenge corporate rule and to insist on a more equitable distribution of wealth and power across Canada and beyond.

God plants the seeds of social transformation and waters them with grace. It's up to all of us to help them grow and bear fruit. Community-based businesses and networks may not, in the end, transform the empire, but working with others to establish justice brings new life in itself. It cultivates God's love among us: the dynamic of fellowship and working together is a marvellous gift from God that can transform lives, heal communities and bring great joy. If we only had faith the size of a mustard seed . . . .

May the God of hope fill you with all joy and peace in believing, so that by the power of the Holy Spirit you may abound in hope.

Romans: 15:13

CHAPTER 4

New Dawn: The Cape Breton Giant

JOHN BIRD

*For most Canadians, Cape Breton brings to mind a re-
gion of rampant unemployment and economic stagna-
tion. Yet it remains rich in something which much of the
rest of Canada has lost: a willingness on the part of
many people to help out their neighbours in need.*

*That vibrant sense of community and the commitment of
a determined priest named Greg MacLeod have led to a
leading CED success story: New Dawn Enterprises.
New Dawn is a community-owned development corporation whose enterprises employ 110 people, with assets
of $15 million.*

*On one level, New Dawn, with its finance company part-
ner BCA Holdings, represents shrewd business dealing,
as John Bird explains. On a deeper level, however, these
community ventures represent a forceful response to the
challenge raised by Kevin Arsenault in the last chapter.
"The major issue in the modern world is values, and a
critical area for values is the economy," says MacLeod.
"If the church doesn't present values, who's going to do
it?"*

The year was 1992. One in four Cape Breton adults was already unemployed. Then, out on this mystic Celtic isle, whose economy somehow seems held, like a stinky fish, at arms length from the comfortable and conventional heartland of the country, came one more in a long series of economic blows. The Scotia Rope plant in Sydney's Northside Industrial Park declared itself bankrupt. In no time, it was shut down, workers were laid off, and its assets sold to an American company which was planning to remove all the machinery to its home in Louisiana.

The rope works would become just another chunk of free-floating economic jetsam, bobbing down a swift flood that has been carrying the hope from this island for what feels like forever—washing it out to a vast and indifferent sea of foreign ownership.

Once, the coal mines and steel plants had thrived in Cape Breton, and there was work enough for all—though dirty work to be sure, and dangerous. Those plants, however, were slowly closed down over eight decades or more, and replaced, in an increasingly consumer-oriented economy, with little besides UI, welfare, short-term government-sponsored make-work projects and seasonal subsistence-level work.

Yet this time a group of people banded together and said No to that removal of nuts and bolts and livelihoods, headed for Louisiana. They did two decisive things. First, they worked together to demand the unthinkable—that the sale be undone. Local church leaders joined forces with the labour movement and the Board of Trade. Over a period of months, they literally blocked the Louisiana firm's attempts to enter the boarded-up plant to take away the equipment it had bought. Many of those who held the line, says Fr. Greg MacLeod, included women from Catholic, Presbyterian, Anglican and United Church groups. They placed their bodies in the way of the huge trucks come to drain another vial of the economic lifeblood from their community. Like bulldogs, they stood their ground until the Louisiana firm finally realized that its plan to dismantle the plant was not in the cards.

Second, they bought back the company assets. BCA Holdings, the non-profit finance company organized to help develop locally owned business, hurriedly brought together a group of local investors. Working with the Nova Scotia government, they arranged a deal with the Louisiana company to buy back the plant— and put it in the hands of this local group.

East Coast Rope, as it is now called, is up and running again, and making a profit while providing employment for upwards of thirty people. Chalk up another victory to the founders of BCA Holdings, and of its mother corporation, New Dawn Enterprises, the largest and longest-running community economic development enterprise in Canada.

Recovering a Vision

One of the founders of both New Dawn and BCA Holdings is Fr. MacLeod, the small, soft-spoken but determined Catholic priest and director of the Tompkins Institute for Human Values and Technology at the University College of Cape Breton. The Tompkins Institute, he proudly notes, is named after Fr. Jimmy Tompkins, a leading light in the famed Antigonish co-operative movement. In the midst of the Depression era, Tompkins established both the first credit union and the first housing co-op in English Canada, both of them on Cape Breton Island. Tompkins "was attempting to apply fundamental Christian principles to the socio-economic order," explains MacLeod. "The first Christians lived the concept that we are all one family, that we all have an obligation to one another." Tompkins "wanted to make the economy once again the servant of the people, instead of the people being the servants of the economy."

Over the years, however, the credit unions seemed to lose Tompkins' original vision, adds MacLeod. "They see themselves only as a domestic service, lowering the cost of personal loans. They will lend you money to buy a car, or provide a mortgage for your home, but they don't see themselves as a force to create a new business order."

MacLeod and his cohorts do see that as their purpose, however. Together, they are recovering the original vision of the Antigonish movement, and winning a place for that vision in the current economic order. It started in 1973, says Macleod, when "a small group of us had become fed up with the government's failure to attract industry to the area, despite years of community agitation and organization. We got together to form the Cape Breton Association for Co-operative Development. We had decided we were going to set up businesses on our own."

With one business executive in the group from the beginning, as well as a student, a social worker, a teacher, a steelworker and a housewife, they immediately decided that to succeed they would need more business experience. "So we recruited several more business people to bring the incorporating group to an even dozen."

They discussed many possible business projects, but most were high on idealism and low on practicality. Their opportunity to make a practical start came when a local handicraft organization appealed for help. It had been operating out of several rented rooms in Sydney, and desperately needed more adequate premises. "They submitted a proposal to us to purchase an old downtown store," recalls MacLeod. "We were keenly interested because the craft activity was culturally valuable and appeared to have job-creating potential."

At that point the co-operative association had no money, but thanks to the business acumen on the board, it did have expertise in standard business practices. "The old store was worth $60,000," explains MacLeod. "We obtained a $20,000 bank loan using personal guarantees from board members, and raised another $40,000 through a mortgage with the Credit Union League."

Even with a high level of voluntary committee involvement, the association soon found it needed to hire part-time staff to handle the day-to-day administration. Where possible, it tapped government "make-work" programs to help the projects stay viable.

The association also made a definite decision to adopt an aggressive business attitude. "From the first," says MacLeod, "we decided we would undertake only those projects which could survive in the long term without government help." Another premise was that all business projects had to have a significant economic impact in order to justify putting time into development meetings. We avoided small, personal-growth business projects that had little dollar value and employed few people.

But we also established a policy to support local business in preference to outside business, unless the price differential was more than five percent. And we chose to give our mortgage business to the credit unions, which were locally owned, instead of to the banks.

New Dawn

From the beginning, the association had enthusiasm, energy and business know-how on its side. The members soon realized, however, that they would need to adopt a more structured approach. They met with representatives of community development corporations in the United States, and with interested parties in the federal Department of Health and Welfare, and devised a pilot project with a new name. New Dawn was born in June of 1976.

New Dawn was incorporated under the Companies Act of Nova Scotia rather than the Co-operatives Act, for legal convenience and to allow greater flexibility in establishing projects. It was, however, incorporated under a special section called "companies limited by guarantee." Although the structure may look like a conventional corporation in many ways, New Dawn is fundamentally co-operative in philosophy. The rule is one vote per person and all profits must be reinvested for community purposes. Since, at the point of re-structuring, the Cape Breton Association for Co-operative Development owned over $200,000 worth of property, New Dawn decided to concentrate on housing and general construction. This was also a response to the expressed needs of the community. They established a large real-estate portfolio offering affordable housing for people of low and medium income. Over the years, they expanded their projects to include a home for the aged, dental centres and a wide variety of job-creation schemes.

The main administrative functions are carried out through an umbrella-like structure providing services and management to many different projects and enterprises. The Cape Breton Association for Co-op Development was maintained as a subsidiary of New Dawn, with the craft school as an affiliate.

There is a key advantage in the founding members' decision to establish various divisions in one organization. Diverse projects can be initiated and all of them can take advantage of the same administrative infrastructure.

The use of business techniques in carrying out social projects made a remarkable difference. For instance, the traditional approach of a community group attempting to establish a group home might have been to use raffles, bingos and other forms of fund-raising to try to gather enough money to buy a house. As fund-raisers will tell you, that can be tough sledding, and not always successful.

New Dawn's approach, however, was to have its Property Department borrow mortgage money in the usual fashion to purchase the house. It would then rent the house to the Social Division for $400 to $1,000 per month. The rental income paid the mortgage for the Property Department, and the Social Division's rental expenditure became part of its operating cost, and hence part of the approved budget granted for such social projects by the provincial Department of Social Services.

New Dawn has been both intentional and fortunate in maintaining a well-balanced board. Over the years, it has included lawyers, engineers, business executives, tradespeople, housewives and pensioners. The basic appeal in recruitment has always been the good of the community. One successful businessman, accepting a term on the board, said that the community had been good to him and he was anxious to make a return. New Dawn also recruited people with special backgrounds to its board and committees. The purchase of a fishing trawler, for example, would not even be considered unless at least one New Dawn member had a strong background in the fishing business.

In the first three years of New Dawn's existence, board and general members contributed more than $100,000 in services to the enterprise. This was rightly counted as equity in the business. If a lawyer undertook the legal search for a property, or if an engineer provided the drawings for a structure, the value of the service was added to the value of the building. These contributions were translated into cash when the building was sold.

In all, since its inception, New Dawn has given more than $5 million in mortgage business to the League Savings and Mortgage Company (an arm of the local credit unions). Its total assets are now more than $15 million. New Dawn quickly became a not-for-profit mother corporation calving a number of independent subsidiaries.

At a community meeting within a few years of start-up, for example, a group of senior citizens complained about the difficulty of getting dental service. New Dawn decided to invest in some "bait" to bring dentists to the area: in this case a ready-made dental facility with $60,000 worth of equipment in a prime Glace Bay location—in a building owned by New Dawn. By offering an attractive, ready-to-move-in facility in a high density area at an attractive lease price, the corporation was able to woo a team of dentists to the area. Their practice was successful and New Dawn had a stable tenant for another piece of real estate.

Encouraged by New Dawn's success in Glace Bay, Westmount and New Waterford both came looking for help getting dentists. This time the corporation got the lease contracts first, then used them to leverage mortgage money to build new facilities. Eventually, the dentists bought all three facilities outright. New Dawn made a reasonable profit while at the same time bringing twelve new dentists to the area.

Not every project has worked as well as that one, of course, and sometimes, it seems, the government has undercut the corporation's efforts, as when New Dawn attempted to develop a gypsum plant on the island in the late 1980s. Outside companies had been mining gypsum in Cape Breton for nearly a hundred years, and transporting it to the U.S. where it was turned into gyproc (or wallboard), some of which was sold back to Nova Scotia. Why not, thought the New Dawn board, turn the gypsum into gyproc right in Cape Breton, and keep the jobs at home? They formed a committee which included engineers, a mine owner, a construction company owner and financial specialists, and hired a consultant from Halifax to help them draw up a business proposal.

While New Dawn spent considerable time and money on the project, the provincial government alternated between encouraging them and wooing large multinational companies. Government officials, says MacLeod, seemed to think such a business could only function as a subsidiary of a major multinational company with already established market contacts. Interestingly, he adds, the government's main advisers in the whole process were those same multinational companies.

In the end the government signed an agreement with Louisiana Pacific to set up the wallboard plant near Port Hawkesbury. Said the July 23, 1991 *Halifax Chronicle Herald:* "Louisiana Pacific Canada Limited has landed a $12 million government loan to complete the expansion of its Point Tupper wallboard plant."

Still, the fact that New Dawn was even considering tackling such a major project—and being taken seriously by the government—shows how important a player this CED conglomerate has become in the local economy. This was brought home even more strongly in the same period when the federal government announced closure of its radar base near Sydney. Another blow to Cape Breton, the closure would mean the loss of more than a hundred jobs. Never ones to lie down and give up when they are kicked, local community leaders began to consider how they might put to use the base facility, with its drill sheds and more than a hundred wooden buildings. They turned to New Dawn as the only local structure with the capacity to take on a project of this size.

A Real Business

"Even though New Dawn has more assets than most of the traditional businesses in the area," says MacLeod, "it has taken institutional leaders many years to realize that it is a real business with a powerful capacity to take on new projects, and not simply recreational play for some bored business people." Because New Dawn is a community-based economic corporation, he adds, other community groups have felt comfortable coming to it with proposals for various parts of the facility, including a curling rink, a centre for a bridge club, and a labour union service centre.

In addition, New Dawn has used some of the existing duplex housing for a planned decentralized home-care enterprise. The home-care project was already in the works, initiated in response to the needs of an ageing population encountering a provincial freeze on nursing home beds. The plan called for a decentralized system of home care with two or three senior-care clients boarded in each of a series of private homes, with one staff person to supervise every ten units.

Other New Dawn projects, all created under the flexible umbrella-like structure as semi-independent children of New Dawn, have included an inn, a plumbing company, a radio station, a "step-on guide service for tour buses," Events Cape Breton to promote the music and culture of the island, a diaper business, New Day Auto Repair, a Volunteer Resource Centre, a commercial centre housing a credit union, library and small businesses as tenants, and even the publishing of a local composition—Song for the Mira—which later became a hit for Anne Murray.

Most of these enterprises have been successful. The ones that have not illustrate one of the central sticking points for those attempting community economic development—the need for a locally controlled source of venture capital. Neither the banks nor, sadly, the credit unions seem able to provide the kind of financial support needed for local development, says MacLeod. So he became instrumental in establishing two loan institutions to fill that gap: BCA Holdings and BCA Venture Capital. BCA stands for Banking Community Assets. "It's a new kind of bank," he says, adding that it is a not-for-profit company. "It's a business expression of the credit union concept."

Beyond Ideology and Technocracy

MacLeod, it seems, is no respecter of structures. His main aim is to create business enterprises that succeed and that meet community needs for employment and for social and cultural services. Co-operatives and worker-owned companies are the ideal, but if a private company, even a for-profit company seems more likely to be successful in a specific instance, then that's what it will be. "Sometimes it's tough to make the co-operative structures work. It takes more human resources to organize them because they are non-conventional. And the workers are used to just having a job and being part of a union; sometimes that's all they want." To change all that, he adds, will take a major, long-term educational program, and New Dawn doesn't have anything like that in place—yet. On the other hand, BCA's future plans are to support only projects in which the workers are the shareholders. "We need to get beyond having the workers on one side of the table and capital on the other."

Neither is MacLeod a respecter of ideologies. "Communism and capitalism are irrelevant words," he asserts with finality. He claims we are living in a world that is becoming increasingly polarized. On one end of a continuum, he says, you find the metropolitan areas, based on a post-industrial technocratic system. "It's mechanistic," he explains. "It's based on pure market forces guided by quantity numbers. The sole decision-making factor is numbers." A metropolitan area, he explains, is any city of more than about two hundred thousand people concentrated within a four-hundred-square-mile area where provincial and federal governments are found. By this definition, only Halifax would qualify in Nova Scotia. "Tory, Liberal or NDP, they are all the same to me," he says.

At the other end of the continuum are the non-technocratic societies, based on human communitarian values. "You find them in developing countries or outside the metropolitan areas." It's a spectrum, he adds. In Canada, Ottawa and Toronto are where the ultimate technocratic systems are found. Indigenous communities in the north would be at the other end of the spectrum, the ultimate

Canadian examples of communitarian values. Cape Breton is somewhere in between, but certainly on the communitarian end of things.

No matter what structure or procedure one chooses for achieving a purpose, its success or failure will often depend upon the quality of the people. Technical ability without moral purpose will not lead anywhere. Moral purpose without technical ability is incapable of getting anything done.

The mere fact that a community corporation like New Dawn has survived twenty-four years, should indicate that serious business can be undertaken in an efficient manner, even though it is for community good rather than the financial profit of the board, a few individuals or a special interest group.

It is, indeed, a remarkable achievement.

CHAPTER 5

Edmonton Recycling Society: Mixing a Mission with Bottom-line Success

JOHN BIRD

Shifting from Cape Breton to Edmonton involves more than a lengthy journey across much of the country. Here in Canada's free enterprise heartland is a business which shows that it is possible to run a profitable business while protecting the environment, offering jobs to disadvantaged people, even giving them a voice in the business, and boosting the local economy. A sense of family is at the core of the Edmonton Recycling Society, as its executive director Cornelius Guenter notes. Its story provides a heartening example of what is possible when people are put at the centre of a business. As John Bird explains, a commitment to human values has paid off for the ERS. It all began with the support of two Christian groups, the Mennonite Central Committee and Citizens for Public Justice.

It's 8 a.m. in Edmonton on a fine, spring mid-week morning. Already the workers at the Edmonton Recycling Society (ERS) are hard at work. ERS trucks are spreading across the northern half of the city, the Society's contracted collection area, as the drivers begin the first of the four hundred blue-box pickups they each average daily.

The drivers are at the front end of a labour-intensive sorting and processing procedure for the city's recyclable household waste. They separate the contents of each blue box by hand into four different compartments as they fill their trucks. Meanwhile, back at the plant, other workers are sifting through small mountains of material to pick out the corrugated cardboard. Still others are stationed at conveyor belts, deftly sorting milk cartons, newspapers and plastic from the swiftly flowing river of waste. Down on the plant floor, a young man manoeuvres a forklift to shift huge bales of paper and containers of crushed glass and shredded cans, all of it destined for recycling at a variety of destinations in Edmonton and vicinity.

It's not glamorous work, acknowledges Cornelius Guenter, executive director of ERS throughout its nine-year history. But the workers here are going at it with a surprising will and commitment. Their enthusiasm becomes even more impressive when you learn that many of them came to ERS with social, emotional or developmental problems. They were classified "severely employment disadvantaged," says Guenter. "They had poor work records and had rarely stayed at one place for any length of time. Now," he adds with understated pride, "they are staying here four to seven times as long as the industry standard. We think this indicates they are pleased to be here."

For People and Profit

One reason they are pleased—and committed—is that ERS, a non-profit corporation, is "their company." It's wholly worker-run. "This company is really what the employees want it to be" is how Guenter explains it. The Edmonton Recycling Society is one of Canada's most impressive CED success stories. A charitable organization, it was formed in 1988 by two Christian groups, the Mennonite Central Committee (MCC) and Citizens for Public Justice (CPJ). Their mission was to "conserve creation and create employment," especially for those left out of the mainstream economy. Their immediate intention was to win the City of Edmonton's blue box recycling contract in 1988.

At first city council was reluctant, because ERS required some start-up capital, and because its bid was higher than the competition's. But MCC provided the necessary loan guarantees, and a Mennonite insurance company put up a letter of credit, in lieu of the performance bond required by the city.

In the end, the Society's non-profit status, an offer to share net earnings with the city, and a commitment to hire disadvantaged employees won political support. ERS was awarded a contract to collect, process and market half of Edmonton's household pick-ups of recyclable material. Nine years later, MCC and CPJ have withdrawn from involvement completely, as their support is no longer required. ERS has been re-structured as a worker-governed non-profit corporation, and it's still growing. By January 1997 the Society had eighty-two employees, had branched out beyond its city contract to a long-term arrangement with the giant paper manufacturer, Weyerhauser, and was in the process of bidding on a contract to build a new recycling facility for the city.

"We have been selected as one of the six finalists to bid on the city's new Materials Recovery Facility," explains Guenter. "It's an $8 to $12-million plant. It won't be easy for us, but we're ready for it." Although ERS is a non-profit corporation, from the beginning "we wanted to show people that such an organization could show business savvy, too. We are motivated by humanitarian cause and driven by profit." ERS has successfully mixed a number of social and economic goals in a way that is an inspiration to supporters of CED:

♦ It provides an environmental service, recycling household waste.

♦ It provides employment to disadvantaged people.

♦ It models a more just way of running a business, namely worker governance in a supportive atmosphere that even includes an in-house counsellor.

♦   It operates without grants, as a successful business committed to excellence, and earns top dollar for the high quality of its recycled material.

♦   It contributes significantly to Edmonton's economy by following a policy of buying and selling locally whenever possible.

♦   It actually returns revenue to the city, with a unique profit-sharing arrangement. Between 1989 and 1995 ERS returned more than $2.48 million to the city from operating surpluses.

Guenter spent twenty years as a school teacher and then several years in the private sector before ending up unemployed. He offered his services to MCC as a volunteer just as ERS was getting off the ground and was asked to help set the program up. Soon he became an employee. Nine years later and still going strong, he says running ERS has been "the most satisfying and rewarding experience of my life. It's an opportunity to bring all my experience into focus in an area that combines humanitarian concern with business."

Good business practice, he maintains, is also good social practice, and "the business community is going to have to face that reality. If, as a business, you don't have good social practice, eventually you won't have a market. Our retailing sector is hurting because of uncertainties in employment. We have been sacrificing work at the altar of technology."

Like a Healthy Family

Perhaps the most fascinating aspect of ERS is the way it looks after its employees, and the heartening fact that a commitment to human values has had positive economic spin-offs for the company. "Many of us at ERS have problems that are larger than we can solve alone," says Guenter. So early on, the Society engaged the services of Peter Rempel, a pastor in the Mennonite Brethren Church with years of experience as a counsellor. Among other things, Rempel spent two decades running a youth orientation program for young offenders.

Rempel comes into the plant two or three days a week, and is available on demand. "If the employee has a weighty personal problem, the supervisor will take him off the floor and send him to Peter," says Guenter. "Peter works with the person to do whatever has to be done. Often it just means giving him a chance to let it all hang out."

"On average," says Rempel, "I see ten to fifteen people a week. Some of them come in with very definite problems that stem from home, as well as problems that come up on the job: problems with anger, dealing with co-workers, all types of domestic affairs. They need a lot of encouragement. Their supervisors wouldn't have time to deal with their personal problems."

"It takes the pressure off," explains Guenter. "It's amazing what it does. We do it for compassionate reasons, but the spin-off is positive economics. The social and spiritual benefits are somewhat intangible, but you can feel the positive morale here."

The service is available to employees and their family members, and if the need or desire arises, Rempel can refer the client to a psychologist at arms length from the organization. Two are available on an ongoing basis. "At ERS they pay a great deal of attention to their employees, to their safety, their physical welfare and their emotional welfare," says Rempel. "The supervisors are clear about wanting the staff to produce. There is no nonsense: they hold you responsible for what you do. But they are also considerate and have lots of patience."

It sounds like the description of a healthy family, and in a sense that's what it is. "We deal with social issues as family issues," says Guenter. "We have a very strong commitment to our people. We try to cultivate a sense of family by the relationships we develop, by the way we deal with one another in the plant, at work sites, in situations of grief and hardship. We stand with each other whenever we possibly can; that's our desire."

But it's more than a family, of course; it's a business, too. "Second," adds Guenter, "we have a very strong commitment to profitability—almost as high as to people. And in order to be profitable, we pursue the highest quality-control standards in the industry. Put all that together with good business acumen—which we think we have demonstrated—and you'll have success."

ERS pays standard wage rates, which range from $6 an hour at the entry-level to $16 for senior supervisory positions. But the bonuses when the company does well can be excellent. "Nineteen-ninety-five was a good year for us," says Guenter, "and so we offered generous bonuses into the pension plan." These are production bonuses to all staff based on the overall performance of the company.

Smaller, informal, day-to-day perks also help foster the human, family-centred atmosphere of the work environment. ERS expects people to work, but it avoids encouraging competitive situations. "Most of the workers here already have too much experience of being clobbered," says Guenter with a gentle smile. "If you put them in a competitive situation, they melt like butter on a hot stove. But if we say: 'Do an extra dozen bales today and we will buy pizza for everyone for lunch tomorrow,' they respond to that." The Society also provides a monthly in-house barbecue and other tangible rewards, such as fine-dining gift certificates and tickets to hockey and football games, distributed by drawing names.

The benefits are also top notch. "It's a good, family-oriented package," says Guenter. "When you work here, you have no worries about health care and things like that." The package includes protective clothing for the workers, and three weeks of sick leave yearly. At each anniversary, October 31, all unused sick-leave is refunded to the employees in cash. "This very popular practice," says a March 1996 report, "has prevented misuse of sick-leave, reduced overtime costs and provided more than half of the employees with a well-earned bonus." In 1995, ERS paid out $47,000 in sick-leave rebates to forty-eight employees. Not coincidentally, health insurance usage was below industry average. "Our carrier is pleased," says Guenter, "but everybody is motivated to work, and when you work, you are well. We place a lot of emphasis on work and wellness."

Then there is training. All workers in operations receive extensive safety training. Equipment operators get specialized training, and have to be examined and certified by the city's Fleet Safety division. The Society encourages employees to advance themselves into professional areas such as accounting, human relations management and technology.

Such an emphasis on work, wellness and a family atmosphere should not be surprising in a business founded by Christians. Neither should it be surprising in a company run by its workers. ERS became wholly worker-governed in 1994, with a board of directors of seven employees and four "citizens-at-large." After a year on the job, new employees are eligible, if they wish, to become members of the Edmonton Recycling Society, the owner of the business. The only other members are the citizens-at-large. Membership lasts only as long as you are working for the company, or, in the case of the citizens-at-large, are on the board. The employee board members include, automatically, the chief executive officer, the chief financial officer, the chief operational officer, the manager of the plant and the manager of collections. Four of those five must be present for the board to have a quorum. In addition, two other directors are elected from among the non-management Society membership.

The four citizens-at-large can be nominated by any member of the Society, says Guenter. They are then screened and selected by the board for their competency and to ensure that they are "sympathetic to our cause." A great deal of emphasis is placed on professionalism and keeping the roles straight. "You are only a board member when you are attending a board meeting, for which, by law, you are not paid. The rest of the time you are an employee, answerable to your supervisor." The board sets policy and management implements it.

A Unique Success Story

When ERS began, local business people doubted it would succeed as a business if it had to meet bottom-line expectations as well as train and employ people with poor work records. The Society's success, Guenter says, rests on the fact that it provides what the customer wants: low-cost, effective recycling services. Everyone involved with recycling around Edmonton knows that ERS was formed to provide jobs for disadvantaged people. "It's our *raison d'être*. But when we talk to the city, we set that agenda on the back burner. We compete on their terms."

Originally, the Society had to go far afield to find customers for its materials, shipping them to Europe, Japan and elsewhere. "As a matter of survival, we had to flog the markets," says Guenter. "We have the best markets in North America, because we're vigilant." In an article in *The Financial Post*, Ashley Geddes quotes a recycling industry consultant, who asserts that "ERS is a model for recyclers across Canada in terms of its aggressive marketing of recycled materials" (March 11, 1994).

At the same time, ERS has been a catalyst for the local economy, reflecting a "Buy Edmonton" policy wherever possible. The Society designed and built much of its own processing equipment, using the skills of its employees and those of unemployed craftspeople. Now, more than a dozen industries in the Edmonton area are making products using recycled commodities as raw materials. They provide more than a hundred jobs, and allow ERS to market up to ninety-eight percent of its recycled waste in the Edmonton trading area.

The resale value of the materials manufactured from the Society's recycled garbage is seven to ten times that of the sales revenues obtained by ERS for the raw recyclables. That translates into an economic impact in western Canada of $8 to $11 million annually, over and above the Society's own operation.

The Edmonton Recycling Society has emerged as a unique success story, mixing hard-nosed business skills with a social mission. It has provided training and life skills to more than six hundred people. For example, says Guenter, "right now we have some students here on a work-readiness program. They are juveniles, learning how to work, but they are paid a regular wage."

News of the success of the Edmonton Recycling Society has spread far and wide. Requests for information and consultation services flow in constantly from local entrepreneurs and municipalities, as well as from more exotic places such as China, India,

Mexico and South America. "I couldn't count the number of business plans we have helped other people develop," says Guenter. The Society's sustainable development model provides lessons which could be applied elsewhere, even if the particular business model followed by the Society needs to be adapted to fit particular circumstances.

As Guenter notes,

In the past many jobs existed only because of unsustainable activities. This cannot last much longer. The economy is changing rapidly, in part because of the unsustainability and because of the resultant collapse of some forms of employment. The demise of the East Coast fisheries and the depletion of large oil and gas fields are cases in point. Many old skill sets are no longer needed, and employment strategies are becoming obsolete and ineffective.

Our economy and our very survival emanate from the environment. We must establish linkages between employment and sustainable development by providing tools for individuals, policy-makers and communities to take actions that increasingly emphasize and assist in the transition towards employment and sustainable development.

Chuckles Guenter, "My mother used to tell me, 'get a good education or you'll end up a garbage man.'" With a Ph.D., he did, and now he has.

CHAPTER 6

Getting the Church Onside: Riverdale Economic Ministry

MURRAY MACADAM

*Like Greg MacLeod, Allan Reeve is a minister whose vo-
cation is to provide jobs for the unemployed and to nurture community economic action. A key difference,
however, is the way the church in various forms has sustained the Riverdale Economic Ministry led by Reeve
during the past decade. As the saga of Riverdale Economic Ministry and its partner Toronto Community Ventures shows, trying to start and sustain co-operative
business ventures with low-income people is tough. As
Scott Marrato, a member of one of TCV's member businesses, says: "Without the resources that a supportive
community can provide, no amount of sacrifice and hard
work can make an alternative economic venture viable."
Nor is community support easy to find in a big city like
Toronto.*

*Yet that support can be tapped, especially within the net-
works of a faith community. Prayer, funding for salaries,
provision of office space, opportunities to speak to congregations—these are just a few of the ways in which
Christians have backed this daring experiment in ministry. The story of Riverdale Economic Ministry provides
an example of how the church can go beyond merely*

calling for alternatives to the prevailing economic system to helping seed those alternatives, putting flesh on the Word.

Riverdale: for most Toronto residents, this neighbourhood brings to mind tastefully renovated Victorian brick homes, gracious tree-lined streets, the vitality and panache of Danforth Avenue, where fashionable cafés vie with traditional Greek restaurants for the attention of affluent consumers. Riverdale: a fashionable address.

Yet, unknown to the tourists who stroll along the Danforth on mild summer nights, there's another, decidedly untrendy Riverdale. The southern part of the neighbourhood is an impoverished community. Houses are smaller and crammed together. In the summer, the stench of pollution hangs in the air from nearby factories. Boarded-up stores and abandoned buildings abound.

In one of these old, nondescript warehouses on Eastern Avenue, however, there's life, abundant life. This is Toronto Community Ventures (TCV): a unique experiment in getting people to work together to launch businesses.

Walking through the door of TCV's industrial shop, you hear the steady beat of rock music and a hum of activity. People are at work, using a variety of industrial and woodworking equipment. In one corner, a man with learning disabilities deftly operates an electric saw.

A few feet away, surrounded by lumber of various sizes and shapes, Pedda Jungmann is building modern furniture. Creativity is key to Jungmann; wood, metal, stone and glass are the ingredients. His business is new, but he's hopeful about the future. Pausing for a moment, Jungmann says: "When you're only one person, it's difficult to get started. It's good to get together in a community place and share equipment."

Next door to Jungmann, Forrest Gump has resurfaced, though not as the loveable simpleton of the hugely successful movie. Ferris Gump is the name chosen by Sylvia Gempesberger and Mark Ferris for their business, and their craftsmanship reflects the childlike spirit of the movie character. Their main product involves a new twist on an old standby, the dollhouse. Their wooden dollhouses fit together in several large pieces with no nails or glue.

Behind the building, surrounded by bricks, barrels and rusty pieces of metal, Phil Sarazen is in his element. This energetic artist and inventor is spray-painting a colossal hybrid vehicle with huge wooden wheels, a steel frame he's welded together, and a unicycle seat. When you first glimpse this amazing contraption approaching you on a Toronto street, with Sarazen on top, the sight is spellbinding. Over it will go a canvas roof to be painted by low-income people at upcoming neighbourhood festivals in Toronto. Creativity is the pulse which drives Sarazen, along with a deep commitment to street people. He has drawn in prostitutes and other people on the edges of society to work on his various projects. With the help of several street people he has developed an innovative exercise machine which promotes back therapy by stretching and stimulating muscles. It is being tested by the Canadian Memorial Chiropractic College. "People on the streets have the greatest diversity in our society in terms of ideas," says Sarazen, with deep conviction.

Being able to use the shop and other facilities at Toronto Community Ventures is "absolutely wonderful," says Sarazen. "Without a facility like this, most of these projects just would not happen."

Economic Ministry

This is a glimpse of life at Toronto Community Ventures, an umbrella business development corporation that is nurturing fifteen community-based businesses in which over forty people work. They include furniture-making, woodworking, landscaping, home repairs, bike repair and communications consulting. Much of the impetus behind this development comes from Allan Reeve, who works through the Riverdale Economic Ministry, a unique outreach ministry supported by the United Church.

Reeve, a solidly-built man whose zest for his work is almost tangible, got into community economic development after working with homeless people in 1987 at a United Church camp on Lake Scugog, north of Oshawa, Ontario. He began the summer scrounging clothes and other items to hand out at the camp. Hearing about the lives of poor people around the campfire at night convinced him that traditional charity is not enough.

"That kind of charity drains people's self-respect," says Reeve. "It means that Christians get to do all the giving. What struck me after hanging out with homeless people was how gifted and generous they were. The biggest need they had was the need to contribute. Yet they weren't able to give; they were always receiving. Everyone needs an opportunity to give of themselves, to work and gain self-respect. Without work we become sick, depressed and isolated."

As a divinity student at Emmanuel College in Toronto, Reeve was well on his way to ordination by the time he went to Camp Scugog. His insights from the camp, however, along with work in Toronto's inner-city Regent Park neighbourhood, convinced him that he was not cut out for work in a congregation, at least not a conventional church congregation. He challenged the United Church to follow through on their call for churches to put resources towards economic alternatives in their communities. He pushed the church to allow him to do community development work among low-income people, helping them to create businesses so they could escape from the trap of poverty. Reeve called this kind of work "economic ministry."

While some United Church people were excited by Reeve's novel proposal, others resisted it. Some argued that what Reeve was doing was social work or business development, not ministry. There was no doubt in Reeve's mind, however, about the Christian nature of the vocation to which he felt called. "The Word and the Sacrament were alive in the community development work we were doing. I saw the gospel story in the people living out efforts to build businesses through co-operation, partnerships and community supports, often sacrificing their own time and goals to help one another, all towards a higher good than simply their own ambitions."

With support from United Church members, Reeve's campaign for a new kind of ministry was ultimately successful. When he was ordained in 1990, he received the formal blessing of his church to do the "economic ministry" work with unemployed people that he had already begun.

Allan Reeve's well of spiritual strength has been keenly tested many times during his decade-long immersion in economic ministry. One of the first businesses launched by Reeve was the Kleinburg Craft Co-op, back in 1989. A small furniture-making business, it was established to provide jobs for people having a tough time finding work in the mainstream economy. Soon it was selling its chairs in fifty stores in Ontario and even to Japan. As the recession of the early 1990s struck, however, it faltered and ultimately failed. Nonetheless, by then some of its workers had become such keen enthusiasts of the co-operative approach to work that they even worked for free to try to keep the business alive.

As it became clear that the company couldn't be saved, the workers decided to start again with some of their own ideas. What emerged were several new businesses organized under a non-profit umbrella called Toronto Community Ventures.

As new businesses were attracted to the benefits of sharing a shop equipped with woodworking equipment and other resources, along with their skills and opportunities, a new model of community development emerged. Toronto Community Ventures represents people with diverse skills and experiences.

"Rather than a few professionals providing jobs for a lot of disadvantaged workers, we've created partnerships with skilled young entrepreneurs who share our goal of creating a diverse economic community," says Reeve.

Reeve acknowledges that it's been a tough haul over the past decade, trying to start up businesses among low-income people who lack the resources that other business people have, getting people to work together effectively, weathering big blows such as the failure of the Kleinburg Craft Co-op. One of Reeve's key partners in CED is his wife Carol Reeve, who is equally involved in community economic action through OCM Marketing and

Development. OCM helps craft producers and other small businesses to access broader markets and achieve economic self-sufficiency.

The support of church people has been invaluable, says Reeve. "Sometimes I'd think to myself that Kleinburg had been a stupid idea, but then people would say, 'Just keep going.' That made all the difference."

The Church at Work

The leadership and support base of Toronto Community Ventures continue to deepen and expand, something which is more important for Allan and Carol Reeve than any particular contract. Adds Carol Reeve: "What has developed is community. What is community economic development about, if it isn't to strengthen community, whether it be in the city where many people live in isolation, or in rural areas where families and communities are struggling to survive the decline of the agricultural sector?"

A new community needs support from other established communities. For Riverdale Economic Ministry, that sense of community reflected itself in many ways. One critical way was through ongoing church support. Core funding over several years from the United Church-based Fred Victor Centre (formerly, Fred Victor Mission) enabled Reeve to continue his work—unlike the experience of many organizations, which find their funding cut off when they hit their first major failure. Reeve's salary is still largely paid by various United Church sources.

Church support has manifested itself in many other ways. A group of women has been praying for Riverdale Economic Ministry for years. One couple donated their second car for use by the businesses. Another person used a $10,000 insurance policy to co-sign for a major piece of equipment. United Church congregations invited Allan and Carol Reeve to speak to their members about their work and to sell products such as Kleinburg chairs to church members. Some congregations made church office space available to Riverdale Economic Ministry. Volunteers helped in many ways, doing accounting, photography and advising on products.

Being a very different type of minister has given Reeve new opportunities for evangelism. After learning that Reeve was a minister, one supplier of nuts and bolts kept making special trips to the Toronto Community Ventures warehouse simply to talk about theology with Reeve.

"Toronto Community Ventures sprang up from a vision of what community could be," says Reeve. "I often call our shop on Eastern Avenue my 'church.' It is a church because people gather here to express their spirituality and meet their spiritual needs. The act of coming together around a common effort is a Spirit-filled activity. When I see people putting aside their own priorities and taking up their neighbours', I am humbled much more profoundly than words can tell by a spirit expressed in action."

Forty people work in the various businesses at the TCV Enterprise Centre. Many businesses consist of one- or two-person operations. There are exceptions, however, and the Urban Sawmill Worker Co-op stands out among them.

This business grew out of a vision shared by members of a refugee resettlement house called Brottier House, Riverdale Economic Ministry, and members of Toronto's Catholic Worker community. "We wanted to be part of something radically different, that would empower people rather than simply patch the wounds created by the prevailing economic order," says co-op member Scott Marrato. That radically different alternative is a business which reclaims saw logs from sites throughout Metro Toronto and transforms them into lumber, most of which is sold to a wholesaler. From modest beginnings in 1992, the Urban Sawmill grew into a business employing sixteen people by 1995, some of them refugees with little or no work experience in Canada aside from the exploitive "temp" agencies. All members earned the same hourly wage and key decisions were made by the full membership.

"In our experience, what makes community economic development possible is real outside support," says Marrato. That support took various forms: loan guarantees from generous supporters; space, equipment and advice from TCV; and faith communities that sustained members in the early days when pay-cheques were few and far between.

"Without the resources that a supportive community can pro-vide, no amount of sacrifice and hard work can make an alternative economic venture viable," says Marrato. "By making time and re-sources available to such enterprises, supporters can encourage a model of development that empowers workers, gives hope to peo-ple, and manifests the real gospel spirit of solidarity in the world."

In 1996, however, the Urban Sawmill Worker Co-op had to close down. It simply could not sustain itself, especially after re-peated equipment breakdowns. However, several former co-op members still work together on Toronto Community Venture projects.

Meanwhile, the wheel has turned full circle for Allan Reeve. He's back where he was a decade ago, at the United Church camp at Lake Scugog. Yet this time he's not alone. Toronto Community Ventures scored a major victory by being hired by the Toronto United Church Council to retrofit and renovate the camp into a year-round facility. That will provide work for a dozen people for the next several years, including some former Urban Sawmill co-op members. This contract provides yet another example of how the institutional strength of the United Church is being used to bol-ster a CED organization.

"It's just amazing," marvels Reeve. "I'm excited to go back, ten years later, with the original vision I caught at Scugog now a liv-ing, growing reality."

CHAPTER 7

Kagiwiosa Manomin:
A First-Nation CED Project

JOHN BIRD

Our next glimpse into one of the many forms which local economic action can take sends us into the rugged land of the Wabigoon Lake First Nation in northwestern Ontario. Their wild rice co-op is more than just a business venture aimed at creating income and employment in a region where both are scarce. As Janet Somerville notes in her introduction, it rests on a vision of respect for Creation and for traditional ways, even if that isn't the most "efficient" way of doing things.

From a spiritual perspective, the Kagiwiosa Manomin story provides a hopeful example of genuine partnership between aboriginal people and the churches, with dedicated Christians and church-based alternative trading organizations lending their weight to strengthen the enterprise.

We know it as wild rice, this delicious, expensive, specialty grain that grows in shallow lakes and rivers throughout much of the Great Lakes Basin. But to the Ojibway people, or Anishinaabe, it is *manomin*—"Seed of the Great Spirit." For them it has been the staff of life for generation upon generation.

In the Wabigoon Lake First Nation, just off the Trans-Canada highway twenty miles east of Dryden near the Ontario-Manitoba border, its significance to the life of the people has taken a new twist. It has become the basis of a community economic development initiative, important in the movement towards recovering political sovereignty. Andrew Chapeskie, founder and director of the Kenora-based Taiga Institute for Land, Culture and Economy, has worked extensively with Joe Pitchenese and the Wabigoon First Nation on the manomin project. "Joe understands," says Chapeskie, "that if you don't have control over your economic destiny, then you have control over nothing."

Pitchenese grew up with manomin. Like many in his Wabigoon Lake community, every September his family would go out on the water to harvest the rice. The traditional method involved paddling a canoe into the thick growth while a second person used a stick to sweep the seed-laden heads of the tall grasses over the gunwales and another stick to tap the ripe seeds into the canoe.

After the harvest, he says, the family processed the rice, parching it in an iron kettle over a slow fire, then "dancing" it with soft mocassined feet to remove the hard outer husks. "It was always the diet during the winter. You cooked it with whatever you had: meat, poultry, ducks."

Most of what the Pitchenese family harvested was for their own consumption. "If they had any surplus," he says, "they would sell it—in those days to the Hudson's Bay store or other local stores."

Then, in the 1960s, wild rice became more popular, and therefore more commercially interesting. American buyers began to come north to purchase the green rice from the Anishinaabe, taking it back for processing in large plants south of the border and then marketing it world-wide. The Anishinaabe were encouraged to become pickers only, suppliers of green rice to a non-aboriginal industry.

As the demand increased, the Ministry of Natural Resources also began to place controls of its own on the picking, granting licences for a plant that was never theirs to regulate. Many of the harvesting licences went to non-Anishinaabe harvesters.

Commercial strains of the wild rice were also developed, and in 1978, they were introduced to existing white rice paddies in California. According to one source, paddy producers in California and Minnesota now account for nearly sixty percent of the world production of "wild" rice.

Pitchenese's dad, Paul, was the manomin boss in the Wabigoon community, the person entrusted by virtue of his experience and wisdom with the major decision-making around the harvest. He helped apportion territories and decided when and where the communal harvests would take place. He made sure the rice was not over-harvested and that enough was left behind for the animals and birds and for re-seeding.

Contrary to popular non-aboriginal belief, many of the manomin beds that appear to have grown wild across the northlands were planted, propagated and cared for by the Anishinaabe over centuries. They developed a complex system, says Andrew Chapeskie, that "regulated not only the propagation of manomin, but its tending and harvesting as well."

In 1879, white newcomers built the first dam on the Wabigoon River watershed, in order to "improve" navigation. More were to follow. Over the years, water levels in the Wabigoon harvesting area rose by almost three metres, destroying many of the traditional beds. So the people found other places to spread the manomin and developed new beds. Their care for the land continues today, still much disrupted and threatened by the continuing social and political effects of colonization.

Back in the 1960s, when Paul Pitchenese began looking at ways to stem the tide of commercialism, he wanted to keep some of the work and the money in the community, and to keep his people involved in the life of the manomin as they have been for centuries. He built a small plant for processing. "It was just makeshift stuff, but it did the job," recalls his son Joe.

Paul Pitchenese died in 1974 and Joe inherited something of his father's role in the community. He also had to earn his position by demonstrating knowledge, wisdom and leadership. "I'm always the guy who wants to improve on something," he chuckles. "I learned from everybody. Dad and I would often disagree; he would do things his way, and I would do them my way. It's been a long haul for us."

Long haul, indeed, but like his father before him, Joe Pitchenese is now the rice boss for the Wabigoon community. He has carried on his family's tradition in a somewhat modified form, adapted to different times—by founding and running Kagiwiosa Manomin, a worker-owned co-operative for the Anishinaabe people of Wabigoon Lake First Nation to process and market their own manomin. "We had become just the suppliers of the raw product and that was the end of the game for us," he said.

The Business of Wild-crafting

The 100-by-120-foot steel building that houses Kagiwiosa Manomin sits on the shore of the Kagiwiosa River, on the edge of the Wabigoon community. Built in 1987, the same year that Kagiwiosa Manomin was legally incorporated as a worker co-op, it houses seven wood-fired roasters. Like oversized cement mixers, they tumble the manomin as it parches. The roasters were designed by Eric Rempel of the Mennonite Central Committee (MCC) to emulate the traditional process as closely as possible, slow cooking the rice over poplar fires. As tumblers have replaced the wooden paddles that once stirred the rice in iron kettles, so rubber beaters have replaced the mocassined feet that once danced the husks from the kernels. Yet the poplar fires still give a smoke flavour to the rice. They also provide employment for local Anishinaabe woodcutters. The propane and electric roasters that most processors use do neither.

The ten-year-old plant is capable of handling up to 500,000 pounds of green wild rice a year, says assistant manager James Kroeker. Production is now up to about 160,000 pounds a year. One pound of green rice produces half a pound of finished rice.

"What Joe (Pitchenese) wanted," says Kroeker, "was to put out rice as close as possible to hand-processed manomin." Other processors, he explains, add water to their green rice, then leave it in the sun to sour and ferment before cooking, threshing and winnowing it. "That makes it uniformly black and hard," says Kroeker, so there is less breakage, and the shiny colour has more appeal on the shelves. "But Joe wanted to put out manomin he can take pride in, and that has roots in the community." Kagiwiosa Manomin's grain cooks much more quickly and, even more important, tastes better.

It is also certified organic, something that most other commercial enterprises can no longer claim, as the use of fertilizers, pesticides and herbicides becomes more common. Nearly sixty percent of the so-called wild rice harvest now consists of hybrid varieties produced on North American mega-farms, particularly in Minnesota and California, says German natural foods researcher Verene Krieger.

Perhaps most important, Kagiwiosa Manomin has allowed Anishinaabe families to maintain part of their traditional, natural wild-crafting lifestyle, which includes woodcutting, guiding, trapping, fishing and berry-picking, as well as the care and harvesting of manomin. Every year, the co-op pays out between $70,000 and $100,000 to buy green manomin from up to three hundred Anishinaabe harvesters, not just from Wabigoon, but from other communities too: Shoal Lake, Northwest Angle, Osnaburgh, and even as far away as Fort Alexander on Lake Winnipeg. Kagiwiosa Manomin pays about one dollar a pound for the green rice, significantly more than other buyers.

All but ten or so of these pickers still use the traditional canoe collection method, in areas set aside for that kind of harvesting, says Kroeker. "You can go through the same crop up to six or seven times in the year." Elsewhere the rice is increasingly collected by flat-bottomed or pontoon boats driven by air propellers. They skim their way through the beds with a beater bar leading the way to knock ripe grain into an aluminium collection tray. It's more hi-tech, more capital intensive, and can often mark the beginning of the slippery slope to the increasing use of hybrids and chemicals to maximize the harvest even in the so-called wild beds. The ten harvesters who use power boats, for example, bring in more manomin to Kagiwiosa Manomin than the other two hundred and ninety canoe harvesters combined.

A competitive harvest, maximized for short-term gain, is not the Anishinaabe way, says Joe Pitchenese. "Manomin carries the memories and experience of our people . . . . When the Anishinaabe people treat the manomin with proper respect, then manomin responds by giving itself up for the sustenance and livelihood of the people."

The worker co-op structure used in Kagiwiosa Manomin may be as close to the Anishinaabe way as is presently possible within the Canadian law which governs economic enterprises. It's non-profit and co-operative, and it's not band-owned, which are all good things according to Pitchenese. "We don't have a whole bunch of members," he says. "There are only about a dozen in the operation, which is manageable. The guys who participate in it are the ones who have the say in it.

"I've seen other operations that were band-owned and band-controlled," he adds. "It doesn't work." With shared, personal ownership, explains Pitchenese, "everything is taken care of and well looked after." With a band-run operation, there is more distance from individual responsibility and more abuse of equipment, he says. Band councils are part of the colonial legacy. They can be very polarized, and power can shift from one pole to the other every couple of years, at election time.

This workers' co-operative structure has been adopted because it creates the least conflict with traditional Anishinaabe wild-crafting relationships, which, according to Chapeskie, continue to form communally around extended family groups. Relationships and duties are defined by custom. He may be the manager of Kagiwiosa Manomin, but "the authority that Joe Pitchenese exercises in relation to manomin," says Chapeskie, "has developed in the context of practising customary livelihood activities on the land."

Support from the Churches

Some of the churches of Canada have long been part of the colonization process in their relations with the First Nations, working in an increasingly uneasy relationship with the government and mainstream society, particularly in the residential schools program. So it is fitting, now that they have begun to understand their mission as one of solidarity with the First Nations, that some of them have been able to provide important support and advocacy roles in the development of Kagiwiosa Manomin.

"In the early '80s," says Kroeker, "MCC began to work together with the band to secure access to the manomin resource. Without that step there would be no Kagiwiosa Manomin plant now. There had been many encroachments, and non-aboriginal individuals were taking over." In the end, he says, aided by the tireless advocacy of the justice-minded MCC staff person, Menno Wiebe, "the community got access to its traditional harvesting areas. They have a community licence with exclusive rights."

"It was a great collaboration," says Wiebe. "It revived the community; it nurtured the old people—without creating dependency."

Still, it's a funny thing to have to go begging to the Ministry of Natural Resources for permission to harvest the rice that your own people planted. Near the height of the struggle, Pitchenese wrote a letter to a Thunder Bay newspaper. To allow "individual licensing of lakes (to non-aboriginal people)," he declared, "with no regard to . . . the centuries of aboriginal seeding, harvesting and caring for manomin stands, would not only be a mistake, but an out-and-out crime."

Mennonite support has gone further than Wiebe's advocacy work, however. Eric Rempel was an MCC volunteer when he did the engineering design and development work on portable roasters that led to the stationary wood-fired roasters Kagiwiosa Manomin now uses. James Kroeker, too, came to Kagiwiosa Manomin as an MCC volunteer. In 1989 he arrived to offer his expertise in financial management, learned at his family's large agri-business in Winkler, Manitoba. After several years as a volunteer, he is now a full-time staff member.

Church-supported funding through the Canadian Alternative Investment Co-operative (CAIC) has also been important in keeping Kagiwiosa Manomin afloat through the difficult first years. (Murray MacAdam tells the story of CAIC's birth in Chapter 8). The plant was financed by a loan from the Federal Department of Indian Affairs' Native Economic Development Program. However, "once it was built the cost overruns were significant," says Kroeker. "We couldn't meet our original terms for paying back the loan, and the bank would have foreclosed."

Fortunately, Chapeskie was able to connect Kagiwiosa Manomin to CAIC, and with Kroeker's business-plan wizardry, they were able to arrange a loan with the investment co-op that they are still paying back. CAIC was "sensitive to community issues," explains Kroeker, "so they renegotiated with us for a longer term."

Churches farther afield—through the mediation of Andrew Chapeskie—have also been important to the success of Kagiwiosa Manomin. Chapeskie enjoys telling the story of how most of Kagiwiosa Manomin's marketing strategy had its birth in a sweat lodge in Karlsruhe, Germany. There, a German *au pair* girl just back from Kenora told the man next to her about this wild rice venture in northwestern Ontario that was looking for places to sell its manomin. The man happened to be Bernard Muller, director of OS-3, a Swiss alternative trade organization organized by that country's churches. Soon Wabigoon's manomin could be found in most of Switzerland's six hundred OS-3 shops, as well as the five thousand "world shops" run by the Lutheran and Catholic GEPA organization in Germany. These alternative trading networks are similar to Oxfam's Bridgehead Trading in Canada, but bigger. They're all part of the International Federation of Alternative Trade (IFAT), whose aim is to establish fair-trade practices with marginalized peoples. "I doubt there would be a Kagiwiosa Manomin today without IFAT," says Chapeskie matter-of-factly.

Pitchenese had already tried to strike a distribution deal with Safeway, but it didn't work out. Safeway wanted Kagiwiosa Manomin to provide their manomin at prices competitive with the hybrid agri-business paddy rice coming from California. Pitchenese couldn't do it, operating on a smaller scale, paying the harvesters a better price, and using a more traditional method of processing what is still organic manomin. Fortunately, the IFAT organizations saw the value of a superior product, and were willing to work through alternative channels. They distribute the manomin as a specialty item to gourmet markets.

With Kagiwiosa Manomin up and running well, and accomplishing its purpose of continuing the manomin culture among the people of Wabigoon, Joe Pitchenese has turned his attention to other projects, mainly the development of a workers' logging cooperative. The logging co-op began in 1992 using both loan and grant money to buy out the band's logging equipment, and to take over their timber-harvesting agreement. That year the workers cut two to three cords of wood. By 1996 they were up to twelve thousand cords a year, grossing more than $1 million, in an operation that—unlike the seasonal manomin industry—runs year round. At peak periods they were employing twenty people.

Yet, as with the manomin, Pitchenese's people are having trouble getting control of the resource they have lived with for generations. They are only able to harvest for Avenor Corporation (formerly Canadian Pacific), which holds the sustainable forestry harvesting licence with the government. The Anishinaabe, despite their proven track record of living in a sustainable relationship with the forest, have no say in how much pulpwood is to be cut, nor where, when or how.

On a smaller scale, says Pitchenese, the woodcutters co-op is also providing wood for a women's co-operative woodworking project in the community, called the Ho-Wa Workshop ("It means 'real great,'" he translates). And with that wood, Ho-Wa is building little gourmet boxes with which to market the rice in Europe.

"We're spinning the dollars around the community one more time before we ship them out," says Pitchenese. That's the name of the community economic development game.

CHAPTER 8

Up and Over the Money Wall

MURRAY MACADAM

*Financing—or the inability to obtain financing—deter-
mines the fate of many business ventures, whether of the
conventional or CED variety. This chapter looks at what
is possible when community-spirited people and organizations devote their financial resources to building a
neighbourly economy. Ventures like the Montreal Community Loan Association and the Canadian Alternative
Investment Co-operative do not merely help nascent
business ventures find their feet; they reveal what a covenant economy can look like.*

*Yet hope-giving as they are, community-oriented loan
funds represent but a tiny fraction of the investment dollars swirling around Canadian communities. The hard
fact remains that most Canadians choose to invest their
money with banks, mutual funds and other cornerstones
of the mainstream economy. This chapter looks at some
possible reasons why.*

MONEY. It's long been identified as the single most important
barrier to the development of small and community-based business. The need for new sources of small business capital far out-
strips the supply.

The Canadian Federation of Independent Business reports that "despite our current climate of very low interest rates and a growing economy, problems with the availability of financing for small business have remained at a very high level for several years." Ontario MPP Joe Spina put it more bluntly in "Financing Jobs and Growth," a 1997 report to the Ontario Finance Minister by the Committee on Small Business Access to Captial: "It did not matter whether it was a farm wife in Stratford, a sports shop owner in Kenora, a carpet manufacturer in Brampton or an MBA student in Toronto, the issue of seed capital is rampant in Ontario." Nor is the situation so different elsewhere in Canada.

The Montreal Community Loan Association

Despite the challenges, some low-income budding entrepreneurs are finding ways to scale "the money wall." With the seasoned confidence of an experienced salesperson, Betsy Thomas ushers the crowd of pilgrims into her shop. Inside, it's somewhat cramped; this is not a big store. We nestle ourselves amidst racks of colourful baby clothes and shelves of diapers. The crowding doesn't matter, however: immediately this place feels comfortable on a warm summer day. We listen with rapt attention to Thomas, a youthful co-owner of this shop. She is telling us about her business which goes by the unique and appropriate name of Bummis. One by one, she picks up the products sold by Bummis: change mats, baby clothes, cloth diapers, describing where each came from.

As the tale unfolds of how Bummis came into being, we see clearly that this is no ordinary shop, and that Thomas is no ordinary business owner. That's why a group of people from Montreal's annual Community Development Conference have chosen to visit this store.

Bummis is in Montreal's Grand Plateau district, near the majestic mountain at the heart of Montreal. Nearby, the vibrant streets are blossoming with fashionable restaurants and shops, for gentrification is making itself felt here. Nonetheless, this is inner-city Montreal, where finding a job is rarer than winning a lottery ticket. That's why the Montreal Community Loan Association was launched. "If it wasn't for the MCLA, we would have been dead in the water," says Betsy Thomas, leaning against the balcony outside Bummis later.

Bummis was started as a small home business by Thomas and two other women, each of whom invested $1,000 for materials. Two of the women were single parents without jobs. Since they had no business experience or capital, banks turned them down when they tried to borrow the money needed for supplies and other start-up costs. The Community Loan Association stepped in, which made all the difference. "When the loan fund approved us for a $15,000 loan, it was like a dream come true," says Thomas. Since that initial loan, Bummis has received two $3,000 loans at critical points in its development. Today Bummis generates $200,000 in annual sales and provides four full-time jobs.

The MCLA is a non-profit corporation involving potential investors, borrowers and providers of technical assistance. It accepts low-interest loans from individuals and institutions, and uses their capital to make loans on affordable terms for individual businesses and broader community development efforts. Since its formation in 1990, MCLA's capital for lending purposes has grown to about $400,000, along with a $100,000 reserve, from a total of thirty-four different lenders. Lenders include foundations, religious institutions, corporations, individuals and organizations. The association's loans benefit low-income people or community groups serving low-income people.

Resto Plateau is another example of MCLA at work. The church of Saint Denis parish in the Grand Plateau area looks like a typical Roman Catholic parish church from the street. Below street level, however, something remarkable is happening. Downstairs, the church basement is lined with long tables. Dozens of people are quietly eating. By their care-worn expressions and simple clothes, it's obvious that most have seen better days. Yet here they are, enjoying a tasty, nutritious, full-course lunch, at a price they can afford—only $2.50 or $4.00, depending on whether they choose to pay the regular price or the "solidarity" price. And while the setting for this restaurant is plain, diners are served with enthusiasm by cooks in sparkling white uniforms. It sure beats the indignity and the bland food of the standard soup kitchen.

Yet Resto Plateau is much more than a low-cost restaurant for the poor. Perhaps most importantly, it provides a ticket into the world of work for some of the many people frozen out of the work world. Since Resto Plateau was formed in 1992, 120 people have gone through a thirty-one-week training program to become cooks. More than eighty percent of these trainees have gone on to land jobs in restaurants or other places. It's a tremendous step forward for people who, on average, had been jobless for three years.

As with Bummis, the MCLA provided a loan to Resto Plateau to help it get started. (Funding now comes from various sources, including government.) It also provided encouragement, so important in getting a business like this off the ground. During those tough early days, Loan Association staff and board members "lent a lot of moral support, when everyone was tearing their hair out," says Chantal Aznavourian, co-ordinator of Resto Plateau.

That encouragement and involvement by volunteer mentors are a distinguishing mark of the Montreal Community Loan Association. Borrowers are involved in all aspects of the loan process in order to build trust and to create a sense of shared responsibility. It's an approach which has undoubtedly contributed to MCLA's low default rate. By mid-1996 the fund had made thirty-eight loans for a total of $342,000. Only six percent of borrowers had defaulted.

Loans have ranged from $1,500 to $55,000, and the size of borrowers' operations range from one-person businesses to a housing co-op for refugees. The average loan is about $8,500. Most loans are made for a period of one to three years. Because the loan fund's investors are willing to accept a lower rate of return—in some cases, no interest at all—the fund is able to make loans to borrowers at below-market rates. "Our investors see the return on their investment as the community starting to develop," says MCLA co-ordinator Carol Madsen.

About twenty percent of MCLA's investment funds comes from church sources. The United Church of Canada supports the loan fund through a $15,000 loan made in 1989, which is being re-paid as agreed. Other Christian supporters include the Anglican Diocese of Montreal, a Roman Catholic order, United Church congregations and the Canadian Alternative Investment Co-op. Nor is church support limited to funding. Church people, such as parish priest Fr. Bernard Morin, work alongside business people and others on MCLA's board and committees. Roger Snelling, executive director of the United Church-supported Montreal City Mission, spends one-fifth of his time on MCLA work.

The Canadian Alternative Investment Co-op

Getting into business—and getting the money needed to launch a business—recently became a bit easier for women in rural Ontario. A loan program launched by Women and Rural Economic Development (WRED) means that women can obtain loans in the $500–$1,000 range. If these initial loans are repaid on time, borrowers can apply for larger loans, up to a maximum of $3,000.

Such small loans might seem insignificant. Yet they mean much, especially for women who may never have received any loans before and would thus have a slim chance of borrowing from a bank.

A network of women from farms and small towns throughout Ontario, WRED has helped hundreds of women realize their dream of running their own businesses, through business training, a loan fund, networking and other kinds of support. The organization's rapid rise in growth and success in helping women launch businesses helped it win an award at an Ontario community economic development conference in 1994.

This women's business network, in turn, was able to kick-start its small loan program through a unique financial institution: the Canadian Alternative Investment Co-op (CAIC). The co-op uses the financial strength and commitment of religious communities, chiefly Roman Catholic, to provide funding for groups working for social change, particularly those involved in non-profit housing and community economic development.

CAIC was launched in 1982 when some Roman Catholic religious communities were concerned that their investment policies were not consistent with their mission. The Jesuit Centre for Social Faith and Justice was one of the key players involved in exploring new options for church-based investment. They came up with the idea of an alternative investment pool, especially to fund non-profit housing projects. The founding members officially incorporated CAIC in 1984. Since then, the co-operative has expanded to represent fifty groups across Canada, with about $4.6 million in assets to invest. And while CAIC is still largely made up of Roman Catholic religious communities, it is slowly making progress towards its goal of a broader membership base by attracting new members such as the United Church-supported Montreal City Mission, health associations and community development groups.

Using funds from its members, the co-operative lends money out at market rates or below-market rates to community groups and co-operatives. No grants are made, nor does CAIC make interest-free loans. Loans generally range between $10,000 and $100,000.

The investment co-op began with a strong focus on non-profit housing and CAIC continues to be active in this area. Another fund invests in mortgages needed by groups developing shelters for homeless people, youth group homes and related projects. The co-op's two funds to support community economic action, a CED Fund and a Venture Investment Fund, have benefited Women and Rural Economic Development, as mentioned, and other CED efforts.

Another major thrust is to encourage organizations that are setting up alternative economic structures, through CAIC's Venture Investment Fund. The Fund has made loans to an electronic communications services network, a housing development association, a courier company and a recycling business, among others.

"The economic situation in Canada calls us to stretch our vision," noted Anne Denomy, chair of CAIC's board, at the co-op's annual general meeting in December 1996. "How do we reach those who need our assistance more than ever?"

Hard times have led them to a stronger commitment to community economic action. "We really want to partner with others working in the CED community," says CAIC staff person Valerie Lemieux. An example of that partnership approach is a recent agreement with the Canadian Women's Foundation to make loans to groups receiving technical support from the foundation, as technical support is something that CAIC itself is not in a position to offer.

The co-op's board members readily admit that CAIC's efforts may seem modest compared to the church-based financial resources that could be made available for CED. What counts, they say, is that this is an alternative that works. As Valerie Lemieux says, the Canadian Alternative Investment Co-op serves as an example of how the church "can be in the vanguard."

The Anglican Community Development Fund

Dillivan Johnson gives the table a final sanding and regards it with a critical eye. Another piece of his craftsmanship is finished and ready for sale. This table will find its way into a Toronto dining room, and its sale will be another step toward his dream come true: running his own business as a woodworker. This dream is a far cry from the frustration of unemployment that he experienced before.

Johnson's dream came about with help from a small but effective loan fund designed to help low-income people in Toronto start their own businesses: the Anglican Community Development Fund.

The fund was set up in 1994 by the Community Ministries Board of the Anglican Diocese of Toronto, with an initial grant of $35,000. Its mandate is to help finance small enterprises, with particular consideration given to people from disadvantaged or minority groups such as women, visible minorities and aboriginal people. Loans of up to $2,500 are available to those with a good idea backed up by a solid business plan.

"We are the lender of last resort," says committee chair Peter Baker. "You have to be turned down by at least two major financial institutions before we will look at your business plan." Loans are made at prime plus half-a-percent interest.

For Dillivan Johnson, getting a loan from the fund has opened the door to financial independence and employment in what he was trained to do, and what he loves to do.

"I had the skills, I had a business plan, but I wasn't getting anywhere with the banks," he says. "When you are unemployed and collecting welfare, they aren't too interested in lending you money. But then, how do you get off welfare?

"I looked everywhere for a job. I was willing to do anything, for any amount of money. I couldn't even find a job for $5 an hour."

While Johnson was eager to do almost any kind of work to support himself and get off welfare, most of all he wanted to run his own business. "I had my own business in Jamaica, so I signed up for a six-week business management course through the Unemployment Insurance office. When I finished that, I started shopping around for funds so I could get some equipment.

"When all the banks turned me down, I was referred to the Anglican Community Development Fund. I submitted my business plan, and waited to see if I would be turned down again."

The committee that administers the fund, however, supported Johnson's business plan and went with him to guarantee a $5,000 loan at a credit union. What's more, Johnson was paired with a mentor, James Bacon, one of the Fund's trustees. Bacon still consults with Johnson regularly about the business and offers advice as needed.

Johnson's sample pieces—chairs, tables and armoires crafted in rich woods such as mahogany, maple and cherry wood—earned a spot in the showroom of an upscale furniture shop in Richmond Hill, north of Toronto. Buoyed by that success and the number of custom orders from the store, Johnson took some photos to the Artisan Guild in Toronto, which supplies some of the city's top interior designers. The owner was so impressed with the quality of Johnson's work that he offered him a job.

"I decided to work during the day at the Artisan Guild and continue doing my business in the evenings," he said. Johnson's Woodworking opened for business early in 1996.

Johnson is deeply grateful for the Anglican Community Development Fund's support. "I had one hundred percent confidence in my plan and I'm a religious person, so I knew there was something better meant for me. The church was there to help me. It is doing a good thing—stepping out to help the community. It has made all the difference for me."

Ann Abraham, another trustee, feels that the mentoring support offered through the Fund is at least as important as the money. "There are ways we can help just by being present to these people," she says. "It helps Christian business people use their expertise. I've been amazed at how they'll go to bat for (borrowers) having a rough time." New kinds of relationships are being formed as affluent business mentors who may have never met a disadvantaged person in their life are now working with them face to face on practical business issues.

As chair of the Fund, Peter Baker says he gets tremendous satisfaction from working on its board of trustees. "For me, being an Anglican is reaching out to help someone who really needs a hand," he says. "This gives me a chance to help those who want something better than being on welfare. And we have a lot of fun."

While it has helped people such as Dillivan Johnson, the Anglican Community Development Fund has encountered some setbacks along the way. A few borrowers have defaulted. Moreover, while the fund has attracted some support within church circles, including a $2,000 donation to supplement its capital base, the example of this loan fund has not been followed, though it would not be difficult for groups of Anglican parishes in a particular area to set up similar loan funds. Nonetheless, the Anglican Community Development Fund provides a model of the way church people in one community can work together to boost low-income entrepreneurs with money, advice and moral support.

These examples show how some people are overcoming the odds to make local business development happen. Yet the sad fact remains: community-based businesses and other types of small businesses need far more credit and investment than they can currently obtain. Their need for capital contrasts sharply with the billions of dollars flowing every year into mutual funds, pension funds, bank deposits and other forms of savings. The Investment Funds Institute of Canada reports that mutual fund assets in Canada totalled $240 billion in 1997, up by forty percent over the year before.

As Eugene Ellmen, author of *The Canadian Ethical Investment Guide* observed at a Toronto conference on CED in 1997, "What's needed are community-controlled funds to attract even a small portion of the billions of investment dollars flowing out of our communities every year. If we were able to re-direct even a few percent of the RRSP investment dollars flowing each year into mutual funds, in a few years our local communities would be able to accumulate major pools of investment for economic development attuned to local needs."

Why can't we attract those funds? The immediate answer is that banks, mutual funds and other major pools of savings and investment funds have tremendous influence and marketing power. Yet we need to look deeper, if we want to come to grips honestly with the critical issue of access to capital.

Overcoming Financial Schizophrenia

As Ellmen notes, "Canadians are schizophrenic about money." When we think about our incomes and individual well-being, most of us think in terms of profit and getting the highest return. And this bottom-line mentality extends into the operation of the mutual funds and pension funds which receive our cash with open arms. Yet when we think about the well-being of our communities and society overall, we think "charity." We give donations to the United Way, the food banks, church projects for the needy and to other non-profit community organizations. We know that these efforts are needed to help those cast off by the prevailing economic and social system.

Community economic development could provide a way to bridge these two separate spheres of our lives. By putting money to work in serving the community, CED ventures can provide for human needs which are now not being met while generating returns for individual investors. Churches could play a leadership role in encouraging a new attitude toward money and investment, one which could bridge the gap between a narrow profit-seeking orientation and the charity mentality. Indeed, the Christian community is especially suited to encourage this new attitude toward our financial resources.

As Christians, we are encouraged to follow Christ in every aspect of life, including how we spend and invest our money. More specifically, the Christian tradition of tithing (setting aside ten percent of one's income for the church) lends itself to the promotion of local economies. For example, all Christians could be encouraged to put at least ten percent of their investments and RRSP contributions into local loan funds, investment funds which focus on small and medium-sized Canadian companies, community-based businesses and similar ventures. National church denominations could set an example by agreeing to "tithe" ten percent of their pension funds for CED ventures. This would give local economic development businesses and organizations a tremendous boost.

Churches and church-based organizations have considerable financial assets, which they tend to invest quite conservatively. The Roman Catholic Archdiocese of Toronto, for example, reported assets of $65 million in its 1996 financial statements. It chose to put almost all ($27.8 million) of its cash assets of $28 million with the Canadian Imperial Bank of Commerce. The United Church of Canada, to cite another example of church-based financial assets, has a $661-million pension fund.

In Chapter 11 we'll look at other ways in which people of faith and others can nurture the community-based economy.

CHAPTER 9

Mondragon: Ideas with Legs

GREG MACLEOD

It's become a mecca for community economy enthusi-
asts, a place which demolishes the notion that CED can
only be marginal. The massive worker-owned industrial
complex in Mondragon, Spain, proves that a commu-
nity-based economy can run head to head with the
toughest competition in the world, and come out on top.
"Mondragon is living proof that alternative forms of
business based on communitarian ideals can and do
work," says Greg MacLeod, author of From Mondragon
To America *(1997). "In an age of disillusionment with*
the dominant social and economic systems, the achieve-
ments in Mondragon have had a tremendous attraction
for reform-minded people in the Western world."

It all started with a Catholic priest named José María
Arizmendiarrieta, who asked himself: "If the gospel
does not apply to the economy, then to what does it ap-
ply?"

Mondragon offers some key lessons for Canadians, es-
pecially about the importance of adequate financing. It
is also an example of the way that modern technology
can be used for profit while incorporating a responsibil-
ity to workers.

"Suddenly, we enter a valley," says Ted Schrecker, "and there's this town—I'd guess of about fifty thousand. It's a pretty, prosperous-looking town. Lots of new housing being built, a couple of nicely kept parks. But clearly a working-class town: no tourist shops, no signs for *pensions* (guest houses), nothing ostentatious or luxurious. And there on the side of the mountain, overlooking the town, are a couple of buildings I recognize from the video I'd seen. So we drive up. No gates or security guards. Here we are at the headquarters of MCC, the Mondragon Corporacion Co-operativa."

Schrecker, now a professor at the University of Western Ontario, is describing a recent visit to the giant Mondragon Co-operative in the Basque country of Spain. With over 22,000 workers and more than $2.5 billion in annual sales, Mondragon is an example of community economic development that attracts international attention. By linking businesses, education and research institutes into one operational organism—with its own co-operative bank—Mondragon has created a remarkable synergy. And it continues to be extremely effective in generating new businesses and jobs. In 1997 it announced plans to create 8,800 new jobs by the year 2000 through new business growth, a far cry from the job-slashing strategy of many modern corporations.

Not Simply an Idea

Besides being an economic achievement, Mondragon is a fascinating social experiment. The total complex is owned by the workers and the customers. Further, the total system is dominated by an over-riding altruistic sense of community responsibility. Schrecker goes on to describe his initial explorations in the town of Mondragon:

> One is struck by how non-flashy it all is. All the buildings are of a modern (not post-modern) functional design. The grounds are well-kept, but everything looks just a bit run down. And wide open. We don't try to go into the buildings, but we wander all around them, taking pictures, and so forth. There are a couple of cars

parked nearby, and we meet an old couple out for a stroll, but no cops or watchmen or anything.

And yet, as we learn later, Mondragon Corporacion Cooperativa is a more important economic player in the Basque region (the whole region, not just this little town) than General Motors is in the U.S. Ikerlan is the only Spanish research firm to have met the NASA technical specifications and hence to be permitted a project on the Columbia space shuttle last summer. Caja Laboral Popular has been rated as among the one hundred most efficient financial institutions in the world in terms of its profit/asset ratio. The Escuela Polytecnica, enrolling two thousand students, is considered the best technical institute in Spain. MCC's distribution branch, Eroski, opened more "hypermarkets" than any other retailing group in the country. Mondragon's capital-goods division, maker of metal-cutting tools, is the Spanish market leader, as is the division that makes refrigerators, washing machines and dishwashers. Mondragon engineers have built factories in China, North Africa, the Middle East and Latin America.

Mondragon is not simply an idea; it is living proof that alternative forms of business based on communitarian ideals can and do work. As the economic crisis in the developed countries has worsened in the 1990s, more and more politicians, labour leaders and academics have begun visiting Mondragon in a desperate search for new solutions. Expecting a community-based business to be amateurish and small-scale, they are often surprised. Writes Schrecker:

> All in all, MCC has a work force of 25,000, and financial assets of about $8 billion. Frankly, standing on the steps of the modest little building that is the general headquarters, it's hard to believe that all this could be true. But apparently it is.

> It's also true that these are extraordinarily hard times in the Basque region, which is in the middle of the deepest

economic recession since World War II. Official unemployment is about twenty-five percent. Indeed, employment in the MCC industrial co-operatives has fallen from 17,000 in 1991 to 15,000 now—though overall employment at Mondragon has not fallen. It's still rare, our San Sebastian colleagues tell us, for a person actually to lose his job. Cutbacks are effected through reassignment to other co-operatives and through non-replacement of retirees.

Mondragon is a real-world example of capital and, more importantly, of technology being used for something else besides the enrichment of non-resident shareholders. Mondragon's successful example is a great help for those of us who believe that the only rational goal for business and technology is personal and community improvement.

To understand what the Mondragon business complex is all about, we must go back to 1956. Six young engineers in this Basque country of northern Spain, inspired by the ideas of Fr. José María Arizmendiarrieta, set up a small enterprise to produce oil stoves. With the help of their former teacher and pastor, they borrowed some money and went into production following principles of democratic decision-making, profit-sharing and community responsibility. They named the enterprise Ulgor, using the first letter of each of their names.

Ulgor became successful quickly. When its owners needed further capital for expansion, they formed a bank, applying the same principles of co-operative ownership. As each enterprise succeeded and grew, they divided and sub-divided to create a complex of related worker-owned enterprises that continues to grow.

The co-operative tradition, rooted in nineteenth-century Europe, is based on the notion of ordinary citizens controlling the businesses upon which they depend, thus making a better life for all. Each shareholder has only one vote, regardless of the amount of money invested. In Europe and America most co-operatives are owned by the customers. Ownership by employees in the form of worker co-operatives is a relatively new development. Thus, when the organizers of the Ulgor company proposed that all the workers should be the owners with one vote each in a co-operative structure, they were breaking new ground in the co-operative tradition.

Although the founders were attracted to the democratic principles of the co-operative business tradition, they were also realistic about the weakness of traditional co-operatives, which tended to be isolationist and marginal to the main economy. To prevent debilitating fragmentation, they insisted that all the businesses they set up should remain linked together as associated co-operative businesses. They have maintained unity with inter-linked boards and joint agreements.

Mondragon has increased tremendously in size and complexity since 1956. In an organic fashion new branches have developed and then branches of the branches. By 1993, the asset base of the complex had grown to $9.9 billion. This is in the range of one of the major Canadian banks. Yet the linkages between branches have been maintained. In order to appreciate the measure of this achievement, it is important to walk through the system step by step, while remembering that the complex began with practically no initial investment. This is especially important in Spain, where most new businesses have been started by individuals who had accumulated capital over several generations.

The founders of Ulgor were working-class people without great inherited wealth. They went to their own local community for money. The unusual result is that we now have a world-class, high-tech, co-operative corporation dependent upon the local community for capital. Mondragon is considered by many to be an international monument to the combined power of community moral support and community financial support.

North American social reformers have been slow to appreciate the value and even the essential role of capital and technology. The Ulgor founders used both in the creation of a new social order. One goal is to use the best technology available in the world. For example, one Ulgor division, the Fagor Group of manufacturing enterprises, committed $18 million to research and development in 1989, which represents 3.25 percent of their sales.

Mondragon's Divisions

Re-organized several times throughout its history and growth, the Mondragon co-operative complex is now divided into four enterprise groups:

1. The financial group includes the Caja (credit union), a social security company, and a variety of para-financial companies involved in such activities as insurance and leasing. The core, of course, is the Caja or Community Bank.

Leaders in the Mondragon system freely admit that if they did not have their own banking system, their worker co-operatives could not exist in Mondragon today. In Europe many co-operatives have failed over the years because traditional private banks were not prepared to support them in difficult times. Mondragon executives cannot imagine a serious co-operative production system without an associated bank. Throughout the years of the economic crisis, the Mondragon system survived while many traditional companies went bankrupt.

The Caja, a credit union, had a clear task from the first to use local financial resources and invest them in the creation of new enterprises. It was fundamentally a social mission to develop the Basque region, which was suffering from high unemployment. Although the Caja began with the double function of finance and new-enterprise creation, eventually it divided and gave the role of business development to another division.

With 125 branches under one board and one general manager, the Caja has become very effective in attracting savings from the local area. The motto "Savings or Suitcases" makes the point that money in a National Bank helps create jobs in Madrid (requiring emigration), while money in the Caja helps create jobs in Basque country.

The owner-members of the Caja are the employees and the associated co-operative enterprises. Each co-operative signs a Contract of Association which imposes strict obligations. In effect, the associated co-ops are not permitted to deal with outside financial institutions. All pension funds, workers' share capital, social security funds, and so forth, are held by the credit union and thus add significantly to the pool of savings from individuals.

Because of its strong equity base, the Caja was able to play a key role not only in developing new enterprises, but in devising imaginative rescue packages when an enterprise was in trouble. It has not been unusual for the Caja to propose an interest write-down on condition that the employee-members agreed to a contribution and a re-structuring. At the Caja's general assembly, Caja employees have forty-two percent of the votes and representatives of the various Mondragon enterprises have fifty-eight percent.

2. The industrial group is the core of the system. Seventy-one different enterprises produce a vast range of products including automotive parts, domestic appliances such as fridges, stoves and dishwashers, bicycles, bus bodies, and so forth. They also do a great deal of construction, including the Sant Jordi Sports Arena in Barcelona for the Olympics, and factories in Brazil and China.

3. The consumer sector is dominated by one large consumer co-operative. Eroski, as it is called, has 264 stores selling groceries and furniture. Ninety-eight stores are owned by the co-op. The rest are privately owned, and operate under a franchise arrangement with Eroski. The chain is the largest distributor of food in the Basque provinces. Non-members are permitted to purchase in an Eroski store, which also distributes furniture produced in Mondragon's factories.

Mondragon exports over fifteen percent of its total sales through Lankide Export, set up in 1980 to promote and sell products, arrange trade and barter contracts, and participate in international trade fairs. Lankide also arranges factory construction contracts in other countries such as China, and co-invests in mixed manufacturing companies.

The genius of the Mondragon system is that it links both the consumers and the producers in one complex organization that respects the rights of both sides of the economic equation. This is in strong contrast to the North American co-operative retail stores, which see their role as delivering cheaper groceries and thereby helping the consumer.

4. The corporate sector includes eleven enterprises established to serve the total commercial complex as well as the wider community. Their role is to promote, assist and develop new and existing enterprises through education and research.

The League of Education and Culture includes thirteen different educational centres, with 6,303 students. Three of these centres are at university level. The largest centre is the polytechnical college, which specializes in production engineering, computer technology, microelectronics and industrial electronics. Attached to it is the new Centre for Industrial Design. In one spin-off from the polytechnical college, students work half the day in a factory and study the other half-day. Education in the sense of skill development and continual formation has been an important creative force in the whole complex from the first.

Mondragon also created a two-year post-graduate, on-the-job training program for management after finding that university graduates were not appropriately prepared for the Mondragon type of enterprise. In 1990, 81 candidates were selected from 1,500 applications. It has a wide variety of in-service programs for managers, such as marketing, communications and finance, and an educational program for directors of co-operative enterprises.

In the 1950s, when the business enterprises were being set up, Franco refused to allow education in the Basque language. Mondragon leaders saw the preservation of their traditional language as a fundamental part of their development mission and devoted a percentage of their earnings to the establishment of primary schools in the villages where the Basque language could be taught. By 1985 there were thirty-five Basque-speaking schools with 35,000 students, organized and supported by the Mondragon co-operative system. After the democratization of Spain, these schools were eventually taken over by the local government authorities. Though they are no longer part of the Mondragon Co-operative Corporation, they indicate an important element in the philosophy of total development. The final purpose is always the integral development of the local people.

Mondragon's Structures

The Mondragon structure depends upon a simple but fundamental principle: alone, each person is weak, but united they become strong. Still, principles have to be embodied in structures. These are some of the major structures:

General Assembly. Every worker-member of a Mondragon enterprise is a shareholder and has the right to vote at the annual General Assembly. Together, they approve the operational plan for the year and elect a Board of Directors. The by-laws require more than one candidate for each board seat so that there is never an election by acclamation.

Social Council. Each department (electrical, marketing, and so forth) elects a delegate to the Social Council, a role similar to that of a shop-steward in a union. The Social Council has no management authority. Although the total money available for wages is decided by the Board of Directors, this committee decides how the wage package is to be divided.

The General Congress. This is the third level of organization in the Mondragon complex and is the most powerful body in the system. It sets down the operational guidelines and the overall strategy. Members must abide by decisions made through the Congress, or else leave the system, a legal option, if not a viable one. A typical rule binding all the enterprises is that no staff member is allowed to earn more than six times what the lowest-paid person earns.

Though all the companies and institutions in the complex were inter-related and inter-linked, the entry of Spain into the Common Market called for a renewed structure that would permit rapid decision-making in strategic matters while still allowing for the development of consensus.

In Spain the Mondragon group holds thirty-three percent of the market for refrigerators and stoves, but in the new Europe it holds only two percent. Mondragon had to consider whether and how, as a community-owned corporate structure, it could form alliances with traditional stock-owned companies. This demanded innovative structures and good communication with the local worker-owners.

Principles Serve People

Mondragon also embodies its principles in ongoing priorities and practices. From the beginning, the creation of new enterprises was of key concern for Mondragon. Regardless of how successful one individual enterprise might be, they still considered it a moral responsibility to create new businesses as long as there were unemployed people in the Basque region. As the Caja grew, they had more capital than they could use, and expansion became an operating principle.

In order to get financial backing, a new venture must first have a manager in whom they have confidence. Further, the investment per job cannot exceed $100,000. Finally, the venture must break even by the fourth year. If it doesn't, then the venture will be changed or rejected.

Another important principle of Mondragon's operation is the engagement of the workers in the enterprise. To become a worker-member, a person must contribute two kinds of assets: first, personal ability, which is tested during a probationary period; and second, a capital contribution, which is normally one year's wages for an unskilled worker. The worker may borrow the money from the Caja or arrange a payroll deduction. The salary of each worker-member is never fixed absolutely. At the beginning of each year, a figure is set which seems reasonable in light of the anticipated earnings of the enterprise.

Any profit which remains after salaries and other expenses are paid is then divided up in a pre-determined fashion. A typical division of profits might be: ten percent to the Social-Cultural Fund to support a variety of programs, from community schools to staff development; forty percent to the company reserve fund, a permanent part of company equity that can never be withdrawn by the employees; and fifty percent to the personal capital account of each member-worker.

During years of loss, a worker's capital account may be reduced. The individual worker only receives this money upon retirement or when leaving the company. After twenty-five years of service, an average worker would receive a lump sum of approximately $100,000, plus a pension equivalent to approximately seventy percent of average earnings during the last five years. This is in addition to a fixed pension, which is separate and does not depend upon profit and loss.

Job security is another key principle. In an age of economic uncertainty, many workers are now more concerned with knowing they will have their jobs than they are with higher incomes. Hence the Mondragon system is very attractive. Although Mondragon workers do not have a legal job guarantee, they do have a moral and effective one—for a life-time. Through zone agreements, workers are able to move from factory to factory. The manager usually prefers to hire workers from the system because they are highly skilled and carry with them a work culture based on collaboration and consensus rather than labour-management conflict.

Finally, a key operating principle is enterprise security: in the Mondragon system there have been no bankruptcies. When a company is in difficulty, specialists from the credit union and the support groups analyze the problem. It may be that they cannot keep up payments on the loans. Then the credit union may propose a solution that involves dropping the interest rate from ten percent to five percent. The workers may also be required to accept lower wages. Usually the solutions require compromise and contributions from all sides.

For the Good of Local Communities

Mondragon can be viewed as a technological breakthrough in the way human and economic resources are organized for the benefit of the local community. On the level of mechanical and electronic technology it competes with world-class corporations. On the level of "social technology" it is vastly superior. It is an example of powerful corporate systems being intentionally directed to the good of local communities rather than to the profit of anonymous and distant shareholders. It contradicts Milton Friedman of the University of Chicago and many other economists who say that the only "rational" guide for business organization is the private accumulation of profit. The founder, Fr. José María Arizmendiarrieta, agreed with the adage, "It is not enough to understand the world; we must change it."

Perhaps it all sounds too good to be true. It did to our university professor, Ted Schrecker. So he kept an eye open for the downside of Mondragon, although he's not so sure he found it.

Its sense of itself as a radically different form of economic organization, as a pioneer opening up new possibilities, that is not what it once was. The woman who showed us around Ikerlan expressed a similar sentiment—but when asked if it was important to be a member of the co-operative, rather than a contract labourer, her reply was immediate: "Oh yes. As members we have job security. And we get to vote."

I'm not as dismayed by the resemblance between MCC and a multinational firm as many are, because I've never viewed Mondragon as the seed from which, by a process of spontaneous multiplication, a new economic order would be born. Mondragon is important because it shows what is possible without capitalists. Democratically structured enterprises can be technically sophisticated and highly efficient.

Observers of Mondragon usually search for the secret formula. They think in terms of a clever mechanistic technique or some novel financial support system. They usually analyze at the wrong level. The answer is found in a category which is better known as a value system. It has to do with how we understand ourselves and our society. It is about choosing one way of life over another.

CHAPTER 10

Fair Shares for Farmers: Community-Shared Agriculture

EDWARD M. BENNETT AND DIANNE HEISE

Across Canada, in communities large and small, people are looking for new, more satisfying ways to meet that most basic need of life: food. These experiments include community gardens, "Good Foodbox" programs, food co-ops and Community-Shared Agriculture projects. Common to them are CED values of self-reliance and community involvement, and a desire to ensure that food production protects the Creation.

Community-Shared Agriculture is a way for people to re-establish a social community around food, based on shared responsibility between farmers and consumers. It's a way to "put culture back into agriculture." The following account of a CSA venture in southwestern Ontario lends itself to a deeper interpretation. As Janet Somerville notes, Laura Reilly's reflection on what it means for her and her family to be part of this farmer-consumer partnership provides "an evocative description of a covenant economy." The willingness to break out of old patterns of "shopping as usual" can go a long way indeed.

How often do people get really excited about the food they eat? Typically, not very often. We want to share a hopeful story about a sustainable farming strategy called Community-Shared Agriculture (CSA), and a local CSA project called the Fair Share Harvest, where people are truly excited about their food. In fact, we are amazed by the enthusiasm and appreciation of the families involved in the Fair Share Harvest.

In agriculture, how the land is used and by whom determines how well people eat and live. The corporate use of the land is contaminating the soil, our food, waterways and the water table, eroding the topsoil, and, in due course, it will drain the natural wealth from the area and destroy opportunities for self-sufficiency. All of this presents an enormous challenge to the security of our food and the survival of the rural community.

Unfortunately most citizens are ignorant of the state of agriculture and the food system. As Brewster Kneen observes in his book, *From Land To Mouth* (Toronto: NC Press, 1993), farmers and consumers alike are being distanced from the way the food system functions, and from where food is grown relative to where it is consumed. They are distanced in time, from when the food was fresh and alive, to when it is consumed, and from the way the land is farmed.

These were the challenges that prompted us to initiate a local sustainable alternative. The CSA concept offered hope because it responded to the crisis in community and to the crisis on the land. With CSA, community values direct the economy, rather than the economy directing the community. It is a food system that begins at the bottom, with appreciation of people and the environment. It reverses the logic of the dominant model of the food system that has proven so destructive to people and their social and natural environments. It serves as a metaphor for empowerment, distributive justice and the value of diversity in the social and natural ecology.

Community-Shared Agriculture (CSA) is an exciting alternative to conventional agriculture. It directly connects the growers of food with the people who eat it in a way that benefits everyone. Participating families (share-members) purchase a share in the farmers' gardens which provides them with a wide variety of fresh, organically grown vegetables all season and a supply of root vegetables for the winter months (an approximate total of thirty-two weeks of vegetables).

It's called Community-Shared Agriculture because it's based on the belief that providing healthy food while maintaining a healthy eco-system is the responsibility of everyone. So everyone shares the benefits of good growing seasons and the risks of poor ones, rather than the farmer alone. The capacity of the group serves as a buffer against the risk of crop failure. Working with many farm families increases the diversity, as well as the security, for everyone. If it is a poor year for one crop, it is often a good year for others. If one grower's onions don't do well, you can be certain that someone else will have a bountiful supply.

CSA is not about providing the cheapest food; it is about providing fresh, healthy food that sustains people and the environment at fair prices for everyone. That is why we call our CSA the Fair Share Harvest.

We live with our family on a small farm in southwestern Ontario. In 1995 we co-founded the Fair Share Harvest CSA with eight farm families. In 1996 it was composed of fifteen farm families and one hundred and seventeen share-member families. Fourteen of the farm families are Old Order Amish and Mennonites. All of the families farm on a human scale, with locally produced seeds and without the use of chemicals. All but one of the families farm with horses. (Farming with horses is not basic to CSAs, although farming on a human scale and with small-scale technology is important to CSAs and to sustainable agriculture.) The family members have among them over six hundred years of experience growing vegetables.

Although we almost doubled the number of growers from 1995 to 1996, the group only permitted a thirty-three percent increase in the overall volume of business. This was to ensure that we could cope with the additional responsibilities. Consistent with the lifestyle and traditions of the Old Order Amish, if the project should continue to grow it will be in small, incremental steps. It is unlikely that any of the growers would wish to produce for a large number of share-members. Instead, the project would grow by adding growers to the group.

Growing Things Family-Style

Working co-operatively by sharing seeds, ideas, and integrating work and social time helps to strengthen the growers' capacities as farmers. Growing vegetables family-style and working as a collective of growers strengthens the bonds among family members and among members of the community.

During visits to the farms, we were always aware that gardening was a true family activity that included even the youngest member. The youngest children often got the job of brushing potato beetles into a pail. Often youngsters had a small plot of their own from a very early age. Family members took delight in working together and enjoyed their work in the garden. Their close connection to nature and the seasons was very evident.

The families rely on the vegetables they produce to sustain their families throughout the year. The gardens are part of a mixed farming operation, and the gardens add diversity and thus security to the farm. Farm families grow the vegetables for between four and twenty share-member families. They say they appreciate the income security it provides, since they know at the start of the season that their produce is sold. Selling from the farm gate is variable, time-consuming and unreliable (especially for those farms not located on a highway).

The growers also say they like knowing that they are feeding families, and appreciate the opportunity to meet some of those families during a farm-visit day. That sense of connection is perhaps the most unusual and meaningful aspect of the CSA model.

Share-members often cite the farm-visit day as a highlight of the CSA experience. They appreciate meeting the families who grow their food, and are reassured to know how their food is grown. Share-members report their dismay at having to buy food in a supermarket with no idea where the food came from, how it was grown, what it was sprayed with, when it was actually harvested (most store-bought vegetables and fruits are picked green and ripen in transit to the store shelves) or what might be the hazards to their family's health.

The evaluations from share-members reveal that many other things are equally important to them, including getting fresh, organically grown vegetables, supporting local farms and supporting ecologically sustainable farm practices.

The vegetables are harvested and delivered fresh on the same day to drop-spots in Kitchener, Waterloo and Stratford. Some share-members pick up directly at a farm. The non-traditional farmer in the group does the deliveries and co-ordinates many aspects. Share-members arrive at the drop-spot and select the box filled with seasonal produce that appeals to them. Surplus produce is packed separately for distribution at the drop-spot. Share-members have often remarked on how beautiful it is to see the rich variety of produce and the care taken in growing and packing the vegetables.

Common to most CSA programs is a group of citizens who are willing to work to set up an alternative food production and distribution system. The Milverton-Mornington Economic Development Corporation, a local citizens' group, played the lead role in marketing the Fair Share Harvest CSA and in setting up the transportation, communication and administrative system. As with most CSAs, this work is voluntary. Interestingly, most members are also share-members and the corporation also includes one grower.

An increasing number of urban share-members is also helping out with tasks as diverse as formatting newsletters to supervising a drop-spot. In a recent evaluation, all of the responding share-members were satisfied or extremely satisfied with the Fair Share Harvest. And they seem to be telling their friends, who are also joining. We were pleased to have been able to sell all of the shares in advance of the growing seasons for 1995 and 1996.

Challenges

Among the challenges in running a CSA program are the false expectations and misinformation that people have about food. Some people don't know what Ontario's food-growing seasons are. For example, there were share-members who expected carrots and potatoes in June because they were being sold in the supermarket.

We grow over forty different vegetables and herbs, and some are novel to most share-members. We find it helpful to prepare a regular newsletter to communicate pertinent information to share-members about the produce they are receiving and how they can use it. Generally we see real interest and openness, but sometimes people are just not interested, and the CSA is not for everyone. In 1996 over sixty percent of the share-members returned, and in 1997 we expected a return rate of over eighty percent. We attribute the difference in expected return rates to members' comfort with their first year's experience with the CSA. Also, we are doing better as a CSA. We work hard to refine and to improve what we do, based on what we learn from share-members and from growers. We do an annual evaluation of the CSA and the growers meet over several days during the winter months for workshops and various forms of resource exchange.

The Fair Share Harvest CSA was launched as a local project with both local and global considerations in mind. The food is grown without pesticides or herbicides, and all of the gardens are verified as organic by Organic Crop Producers and Processors Ontario, Inc. The land is farmed with horses and small-scale technology which reduce the compaction of the soil and increase its aeration. This, along with composting the manure and the use of other organic farm strategies, increases the soil fertility and adds greatly to the health value and the safety of the food. It is a form of sustainable agriculture that is appreciative of the natural ecology.

With an early start to the season made possible by the greenhouse capacity of two growers (who provide the group with early plants), and regular re-plantings of some vegetables, the land can be very productive. In 1996, on seven acres of land, we estimated

111

that the Fair Share Harvest CSA provided approximately five hundred and twenty-five people (based on an average calculation of four people per farm and share-member family) with fresh in-season and root storage vegetables for thirty-two weeks. Families who purchased an additional volume of bulk order produce (at wholesale prices) for root storage or preserving could maintain themselves in vegetables and small fruits for the full year.

All of the farm families and some share-members preserve produce for the full year, and other share members are experimenting with preserving their favourite vegetables and fruits. In 1996, fifteen percent of our gross sales was extra produce for preserving. The volume would have been greater, but we didn't have the capacity to handle it and had to refuse sales.

A Rural-Urban Partnership

The CSA can be created and maintained through a partnership between rural and urban people without government or corporate assistance. The CSA leads to the formation of new relationships, social participation around food, farming and family, and helps to promote a sense of community. There is a festive spirit at the drop-spots and during farm pick-up times and farm-visit days. The meetings of the growers include a potluck lunch, which always feels like a celebration. Community is important to sustainable agriculture and to food security and consumption. The CSA concept is about building community and the Fair Share Harvest helps to sustain the social ecology of the rural community.

Control over one's food source is empowering to farmers and share-members. Buying the food locally supports local farm business and employment and adds to a community's food security. The local markets reduce the distance between the source of food and our mouths, and the organic growing strategies are beneficial to our bodies and to the environment. Money up-front and the volunteer support of the CSA infrastructure allow the farmer to concentrate on growing the food.

Although it is a "small system," Community-Shared Agriculture honours the biological and social principle of diversity on the land and in the community. It is an example that can be replicated across other food production and distribution systems without demanding uniformity and conformity, except to sustainable eco-centric values and principles. It can inspire many successful small local economies and food systems at reasonable cost to the entire population.

An Advent Reflection
from a Fair Share Family

LAURA REILLY

*The Lord will shower his gifts and our land will yield its
fruit.*

Communion Antiphon
First Sunday of Advent

Advent begins as we are descending into the darkest time of the
year. The harvest is over—the leaves have withered and are being
blown away by cold winds.

Not only are we in North America facing the darkness of the
natural world, but we also face the darkness of the market place.
These days, when economic booms are over, individuals' pros-
pects seem to have withered and been blown away by multi-na-
tional agendas.

Somehow the winding down of the land for the winter months,
and the passing of Daylight Saving Time are expected—we're not
afraid of them. The darkness of the market place, however, is driv-
ing many into hopelessness.

In a market economy, money and industrial machinery are seen
as the main factors of production. Natural resources such as the
land are meant to be exploited so that produce is available any time
of year: tomatoes in July or December, for those with the money
to buy them.

Last spring, my family entered a different "market economy."
We joined the Fair Share Harvest. In the face of agri-business, herbicides and pesticides, a small community of Amish have opted
for a simple and natural way of production. They have chosen to

farm small plots of land, without herbicides and pesticides, diversifying their produce and distributing it within their families and to a local economy. Food is freshly picked by the growers and delivered on that day to the consumers—with no need for preservatives or additives.

For me and my family, the experience of Fair Share has been a true sign of hope in a dark time, and has opened our imaginations to different ways of being in the marketplace—ways that do not keep us bound up in fear, but open to the possibility of living creatively and sharing the abundance of gift.

The community of growers enters into a relationship with the land that honours the rhythms of the natural world. This community remembers that nature's drive is to be productive and self-renewing. In their small community, the land is not artificially pumped up with herbicides and pesticides in order to extract as much as possible for now or for as much as the market will bear, without a view to the next generation.

The Amish allow the land to produce a diverse small crop which will be shared. The soil is given time to rest and to be preserved for the next season and for the next generation. The careful harvesting and tending of the land, not the maximizing of RRSP contributions or a diversified mutual fund portfolio, is the true sustainer of human life.

The Amish growers have established a community where hardships and abundance are shared. If one grower has less, those with more make up the difference. This way of working extends to those who buy the produce. We "bear the risk" with the grower by buying our shares in advance of the harvest. The money can be used by the grower for seed and costs of planting. Whatever the harvest, it is shared.

As we receive the produce, we have a deep gratitude for the growers of our food. We see the choices that they have made to live and work in a counter-cultural way that has fed us with fresh, local, delicious produce and with rich food for our imaginations.

Receiving the produce right when it was harvested, I was much more deeply aware of the rhythm of the land. My relationship with the food became not only one of consumption but also one of creativity. I learned to use beet greens and other greens that I had never seen or heard of. Our family's menus reacted to the local growing season—and now, rather than feeling deprived because we can't afford hothouse tomatoes from Mexico in December, we are enjoying the local tomatoes we canned when they were in abundance in late August.

I feel a deep satisfaction in the learning of new recipes and in new skills such as freezing and canning.

This deepened awareness of the natural world and our dependence on it for life reminds me that the Creator desires to shower gifts upon us. In this dark time, we must hear and open our hearts and imaginations to receive those gifts.

CHAPTER 11

Growing the Community Economy

MURRAY MACADAM

We can *get there from here: from what we've got now, to where we'd like to be.*

It starts with believing in the possibility. "By breaking out of the mould of traditional thinking—that economics is for profit, altruism is for charity—it is possible to confront the leaner and meaner economy of the 1990s head on," notes ethical investment expert Eugene Ellmen in The Canadian Ethical Money Guide *(1997). Once that new mind-set has been reached, a whole range of actions can help bring a neighbourly economy into view.*

Could community economic development become a major player in Canada's economy?

While the potential for that to occur depends, in this author's view, on broader social and economic changes in Canada overall, others are more optimistic. For SEED Winnipeg manager Garry Loewen, the answer is clear: "It's a matter of whether we're prepared to develop the will to do it."

That optimism grows out of the rapid growth in CED businesses in recent years and the potential that exists for much greater growth. "There are new kinds of partnerships between poor people and business people, between financial institutions and those marginalized from financial institutions," says Mike Lewis, director of the Community Enterprise Centre in Vernon, B.C., and a consultant to community organizations across Canada. "We are creating some examples where real social and economic value is being created."

There are plenty of ways in which local congregations, parishes, church groups and community organizations can encourage local economic development:

Shift Your Attitude

The first step is to think locally, and to think about what you and/or your group can do to support your local economy. Remember that CED includes a broad range of activities: helping people start new businesses, barter systems, credit unions, businesses with a social mandate. The more we support them, the more we can see a community economy emerge.

We can strengthen that community economy in so many ways. For example, just think for a moment of the various organizations to which you belong: service clubs, small business associations, political parties, neighbourhood groups, trade unions, churches, school boards. Are there not some ways in which you can nudge these organizations and other bodies to use their resources of people and money to support the local economy? As the examples in this book show, all these groups can strengthen CED through buy-local campaigns, barter networks, offering space to community groups—the list of possibilities is limited only by our imaginations. Community economic development is about working together and co-operation.

Remember the multiplier effect: in a healthy economy, a dollar gets spent six to eight times before it leaves the community.

Think Globally, Shop Locally

All kinds of opportunities exist to use your money, and the money of people who share your values, to support community-based businesses.

Buy locally produced products and services first, even if they cost a bit more. Support businesses which combine social goals with business goals.

Join a local barter network such as the Local Exchange Trading System (LETS) found in a number of communities across Canada. Whether barter can move from the margins of our economy to become a major player depends on how many people and organizations get involved in it, says John Phillips, a LETS organizer in Edmonton's low-income McCauley neighbourhood. "Potentially it could do tremendous things to meet the huge gap in the current economy," he says.

Why not follow the example set by Edward Bennett and Laura Reilly in Chapter 10 and become part of a Community-Shared Agriculture (CSA) group in your community, or start such a group if none exists? CSA is an exciting alternative to the way most of us get our food. It directly links growers of food with the people who eat it so that everyone benefits. Members buy a share in the farmers' gardens which provides them with fresh vegetables all season. Buying a share, and thus sharing the risk which usually only the farmer bears, reflects the belief that providing food is everyone's responsibility. The vegetables are delivered to drop-off spots, or members may pick them up at the farm. There's always a "farm day" during the season when members and their families can visit the farm, thus deepening the sense of community among everyone involved. Buying our food can be a meaningful and even joyful experience, instead of a humdrum chore.

Share Your Business Skills

Volunteer to be an adviser or "mentor" for a new entrepreneur or business development group, if you have business skills or experience. As the examples of the Anglican Community Development

Fund and Riverdale Economic Ministry show, your advice and moral support can make a big difference to someone just starting out. Many people have found this experience to be deeply rewarding.

Invest in Your Community

Join a credit union and encourage other organizations to which you belong to strengthen the credit union alternative to the big banks.

The next time you hear someone bemoan the scarcity of funding for community or socially useful initiatives, consider this: 4.2 million Canadians are members of credit unions or their francophone counterparts, the *caisses populaires*. The assets of Canada's 873 credit unions and *caisses populaires* total $47 billion. These are community banks, locally owned and operated by members.

Some credit unions have become indistinguishable from banks. "While sceptics can rightly claim that the Canadian credit union system has not played a major social or economic leadership role in recent decades, the framework is still in place," says Larry Gordon, vice-president of development at Metro Credit Union in Toronto. "Community-based financial co-operatives will only rise to what their member-owners demand of them. If the local community has no special expectations of its credit union, it will probably act no differently than a traditional bank. On the other hand, if the local community pushes the credit union to excel in terms of banking policies, programs and services, then it will do so."

What that local pressure can accomplish can be seen at the 40,000-member Metro Credit Union, which handles loans made under the Anglican Community Development Fund. It conducts a bi-annual social audit which measures progress in many areas related to social responsibility as well as the well-being of members, employees and the general public. The Assiniboine Credit Union, Manitoba's second largest, also reflects a strong community development focus. A key member of a CED network in Winnipeg, Assiniboine is also part of efforts to improve the community in

Winnipeg's troubled inner city. It switched from buying office supplies from the U.S.-owned Grand and Toy company to Friesen's, an office supply firm in Altona, Manitoba, proud to be locally owned and partly owned by its employees.

The Vancouver City Savings Credit Union (VanCity) is a sparkling example of what can be done to nurture community development. After gaining credit union support for a change-oriented agenda in the late 1980s, VanCity has continued to develop new programs for meeting a broad range of community needs. The potential is enormous, since VanCity is Canada's biggest credit union, with 218,000 members and $4.37 billion in assets.

VanCity Community Foundation, launched by the VanCity Savings Credit Union, provides loans, grants and technical assistance for a broad range of community development ventures, such as the Picasso Café, which provides on-the-job restaurant training for youth moving away from street life. The Foundation launched two innovative lending programs in 1995: a Community Loan Fund, which allows organizations and individuals without a strong credit history or collateral to borrow up to $5,000, and "self-reliance" loans of up to $15,000 to individuals for very small businesses.

Invest some money in your local Community Loan Fund, if there is one, and encourage others to do likewise. Various loan funds are springing up around the country providing loans to small businesses, co-operatives, and community-based projects.

If you're a church member, encourage your congregation and national church to devote more of their financial resources to boost CED. As noted earlier, lack of investment capital is one of the single biggest hurdles which prevent community-based economic ventures from getting off the ground. "You often hear people say that CED is just marginal," says Allan Reeve of the Riverdale Economic Ministry and Toronto Community Ventures. "Part of the reason is that only marginal amounts of money are made available for it."

Initiatives such as the Anglican Community Development Fund and the Canadian Alternative Investment Co-operative, while valuable, represent only a fraction of the church-based financial resources that could be made available for community economic action, despite the cutbacks faced by most denominations.

As Jennifer Henry, program co-ordinator for the Ecumenical Coalition for Economic Justice, remarked at the Commission on Justice and Peace Forum held in Ottawa in 1996, "What we urge governments to do, we should do ourselves. We need to look at how the 'justice' church can come to terms with the 'bond-holder' church."

Similarly, congregations, outreach ministries and other church bodies can make funding available to enable CED ventures to get off the ground, similar to the research and development funding and other support routinely provided by large corporations for their new ventures. An example of such "R and D" funding in Toronto was the core funding from the Fred Victor Centre which helped establish the Riverdale Economic Ministry. A $20,000 interest-free loan from the Fred Victor Centre helped launch Fresh Start Cleaning and Maintenance, a business providing work in a supportive setting for people with mental health problems. A grant from the Anglican Church of the Redeemer helped launch All-A-Board Youth Ventures, a Toronto organization working to provide a future with dignity for street youth through job training and work in a café and furniture business.

At the same time, the financial support which the church can offer should not be considered apart from the church's larger vision. Otherwise, as a paper written to the United Church's General Council noted, such funding "perpetuates a stereotype of the church [as a] foundation or a detached institution, primarily concerned about self-perpetuation. Seeing the church committed to community and economic development through its staff, its volunteers and its resources presents a picture of a faith community actively seeking God's justice in the world."

The Church: Taking a Prophetic Stance

The church has a rich bounty of resources—of people, spiritual strength, connections to other community partners, money, church buildings and other property. It has tremendous potential to be a major advocate for, and initiator of, community economic development. By drawing together people from many walks of life around a common spiritual goal, churches offer a vehicle for individual and social transformation rarely found in the rest of society. "Churches are uniquely positioned to do some wonderful things, if they could only get their minds off things like fixing the roof," says Rick Sheffer, only half-facetiously. Sheffer, director of a Presbyterian-Anglican outreach ministry in Montreal called Tyndale-St. George's, is trying to create new ways for his mission to help crack the poverty-welfare cycle in which so many local residents are trapped, by such means as partnerships with local businesses.

The preceding chapters have sketched many examples of ways that church people, congregations and broader church bodies can support community economic action. These can include:

◆ Prayer on behalf of CED initiatives;

◆ Ensuring that congregations, seminaries and theological colleges include community values in their moral and ethical reflections, and in education on broader social and economic issues. As community organizer Joan Kuyek of Sudbury notes, "Economics has been elevated to the level of a religion in our society: it has its own priesthood, its own symbolic language and ritual observances (Christmas, Mother's Day, Easter) and it has a code of conduct for human affairs based on profit and the bottom line . . . . We need to reclaim and rename economics for ourselves" ("Which side are we on?" *Community Economics,* Fall 1996, 11). A good place to start is by taking advantage of the economic literacy resources and educational programs offered by the Ecumenical Coalition for Economic Justice;

◆ Freeing up individual ministers and priests to do community economic development work as their ministry, or as part of it;

◆ Sponsoring CED businesses and initiatives in conjunction with social service agencies and others;

◆ Enabling community groups and community-based businesses to rent space in local churches for free or at low cost;

◆ Encouraging church members with business skills to act as mentors for new entrepreneurs;

◆ Working with community organizations to nurture local business efforts, following the example set by such groups as the Canadian Alternative Investment Co-op and the Montreal Community Loan Association;

◆ Engaging the church, at all levels, in broader advocacy efforts. For example, the Church-in-Society Committee of the United Church sponsored two resolutions on banks at the 1996 annual meeting of the Church's Toronto Conference. One asked the government to urge chartered banks to invest three percent of their profits in small business and one percent back in the community; the other urged the Toronto Conference to switch its own banking business to a credit union, due to the transparency and accountability offered;

◆ Making local church buildings available to community groups, as some already do. Virtually every church building contains a kitchen. Those kitchens can be made available to people who are part of Canada's rapidly expanding number of "community kitchens"—places where people meet each other to cook, thereby saving money, learning new skills and deepening bonds with each other. By November 1996, Quebec had at least three hundred community kitchens, B.C. had at least a hundred, and the number was growing in Ontario.

An example of the way church space can serve broader community needs can be seen in Resto Plateau, a successful CED business in a Montreal Catholic parish, where each day a couple of hundred low-income people enjoy low-cost meals. After a few months at Resto Plateau, most of the trainees land permanent jobs as cooks elsewhere. Similarly, the Church of the Holy Trinity, an Anglican parish in downtown Toronto, makes its basement and kitchen available to Trinity Square Café. The café grew out of a soup kitchen based at the church, and involves a revamped training program at George Brown College for psychiatric survivors, as well as church support for a self-help restaurant. It provides work and training experience for people who have had mental health difficulties and who want to get back into the work force.

Kick-starting Local Economic Action: Two Initiatives

The range of possibilities for community economic development are almost limitless. Here are two examples of how committed church people have made a difference for their whole community. One, from Alberta, shows how ecumenical action can make a difference. The second, from Ontario, is an example of leadership by a committed Christian of a highly successful community development organization.

To the old Edmonton City Council, the idea seemed terrific: open a restaurant in City Hall and staff it with a mix of food-service professionals and marginalized kids eager to learn skills to help them get off the streets. Yet a new, more conservative City Council elected in October 1995 was less enthusiastic. The project was fine, said Mayor Bill Smith, as long as it was located somewhere else.

The business was a new venture for the Edmonton City Centre Church Corporation. Backed by five local churches—All Saint's Anglican, McDougall United, Augustana Lutheran, St. Joseph's Roman Catholic and First Baptist—the corporation offers school feeding programs, housing, a women's shelter and other services to benefit low-income folks in inner-city Edmonton.

The churches realized that these jobless street youth needed more. "Most had complex social problems and educational deficiencies that made getting a job not very realistic," says the Church Corporation's executive director Martin Garber-Conrad. "A restaurant seemed ideal."

When members of the participating churches heard of Council's flip-flop, they sprang to the forefront of a citizen-action campaign to keep the restaurant in City Hall. They agreed that moving the restaurant would amount to a symbolic marginalizing of already marginalized young people. Church members and other community supporters lobbied their councillors on behalf of the restaurant. Hundreds of phone calls supporting the City Hall location were generated in the space of a few weeks.

Council eventually relented, and in the summer of 1996 the twenty-five-table Kids in the Hall Bistro opened. Business has been brisk ever since. Backed by a three-year, $922,000 federal Human Resources Development grant, twenty-eight young people are learning the restaurant ropes on six-month stints. The first group of trainees graduated in January 1997 with flying colours: all have either landed permanent jobs or have returned to school.

Lutherwood Community Opportunities Development Association

The time: November 1995. The place: the Radisson Hotel, London, Ontario. The event: a province-wide CED Conference. And the pinnacle of the event: presentation of three awards for excellence in community economic action.

One award went to the Consumer-Survivor Business Council, which starts up businesses throughout Ontario for people with mental health problems. The second went to David Hall, widely acclaimed for his success in transforming Toronto's Dufferin Mall through links with local businesses, schools and community groups.

George Ingram, an elder in the Presbyterian Church, strode to the podium to accept the third award on behalf of a remarkable community organization based in Waterloo Region: the Lutherwood Community Opportunities Development Association (CODA). It's an independent non-profit agency that helps people find work or create their own jobs. Lutherwood CODA's services span the gamut: employment counselling, job-search programs, self-employment training for entrepreneurs and workplace training centres that help people upgrade their job skills. Nearly seven thousand people are helped in some way by the organization every year.

Lutherwood CODA has reached a scale that few CED businesses or projects achieve, one that means it can have a meaningful impact on the local economy. Over 28,000 people have benefited in some way from the agency's work since 1984. In 1995 the Association helped more than three hundred people launch businesses, opened an Entrepreneur Club and Business Action Centre, and helped more than one thousand people find work.

It all began as a community response to the recession of the early 1980s which battered Waterloo Region. As unemployment hit one worker in five, local church, community and labour leaders set up an Unemployment Help Centre. Self-employment training evolved from the centre. In turn, that evolved into the Lutherwood Community Opportunities Development Association.

CODA's impressive track record is based on deep community roots. One person, however, has made a critical difference: a scrappy Mennonite named Paul Born, who has worked tirelessly as the director since its inception. The example shown by Christians with a social conscience, such as J. S. Woodsworth, Tommy Douglas, Jean Vanier and Henri Nouwen, inspired Born toward community service—and to stick with Lutherwood CODA despite some enormous challenges during the past decade. "The idea of being a minister to society, of being God's church in the world, resonated with me," says Born. "A Mennonite lives out service. He doesn't talk about it." He adds, "The CED model is the best model for creating small businesses."

For people shut out of the economic system, it is vital to create a supportive environment. CODA provides strong volunteer support to nurture people starting businesses. The organization's two hundred and fifty volunteers include over a hundred people with professional experience in translating someone's business dream into reality. This strong community base is a key ingredient in CODA's high success rate. Two years after graduation, ninety-five percent of people who take the agency's self-employment program—people who had been on social assistance—are still working.

Other kinds of practical help are offered. Most small businesses start on shoestring budgets and can't afford all the equipment and support services they need. The Entrepreneur Club and Business Action Centre, located at CODA's small business training centre in Kitchener, fills the gap. It offers group discounts on business products, advertising, accounting, access to computers and other services. Funding comes from community donations, memberships and fees for services. A Women-In-Business network strengthens low-income women, especially single mothers, who have gone into business.

The Lutherwood Community Opportunities Development Association continues to develop in new ways. Partly in response to government cutbacks, it has started catering and renovation businesses. It scored a coup by winning a public tender to run a café at the Kitchener Public Library. Now library patrons can sip a coffee or enjoy a snack served by employees of As You Like It Café, people who had been living on welfare before.

Developing links with a wide range of organizations is a core element of the association's operations. The café business, for example, is the fruit of a partnership among Lutherwood CODA, the Kitchener Public Library Foundation and KW Habilitation Services. CODA's funds come from many sources, including the United Way, governments, the city of Cambridge, fees for services and donations. The agency works with twenty-two other community agencies to deliver its various programs and services.

Lutherwood CODA has had some success in providing the capital needed by new businesses. In 1989 it launched a Micro-Enterprise Loan fund, which offers loans of up to $5,000. By 1996 it had loaned out over $200,000. The Supporting Employment and Economic Development (SEED) Fund, a second-loan fund, provides loans of up to $15,000 to graduates of CODA's self-employment training program. In its first eight months of operation the fund provided loan guarantees of almost $72,000 to seven microbusinesses. SEED's goal is to raise $2 million in investment capital—an ambitious goal when you consider that lenders to the Fund are paid no interest. Yet by June 1997, more than $700,000 had been raised.

Lutherwood CODA launched an ambitious effort in May 1998 to lift two thousand families out of poverty by the year 2000. This Opportunities 2000 program builds on the organization's past success in tackling unemployment and poverty by helping community groups, neighbourhoods and individuals develop job training and businesses. For example, the Food Bank of Waterloo Region is working with the help of Opportunities 2000 to transform some of its collective kitchens into specialty food businesses employing low-income people.

"We want to be the leaven in the community," says Paul Born. "Through example, people will accept that CED is a real alternative."

Yet he would like the church to become more involved in supporting the Lutherwood Community Opportunities Development Association and its various initiatives. Many CODA volunteers are Christians who help because of their faith understanding. "The church recognizes the importance of work and economic development in developing countries," notes Born. "Why is it so silent about CED in Canada?"

Seeds of New Life

This book started with a quote from the Book of Revelation for good reason. As Canada approaches the millennium, we urgently need new ways of living, especially in the way we earn our daily bread. How many of us are denied that opportunity altogether? It is incredible that a country as bountiful as ours quietly resigns literally millions of its citizens to the humiliation and hardship of food bank line-ups, the isolation of unemployment, the limbo existence of a shelter instead of a real home, the insecurity of worrying whether they'll still have a job next year or next month.

The solutions to poverty and unemployment are not easy, but they can start with an acknowledgement of two important facts which often get ignored these days. First, we're all in this together. Second, we need to think about the impact of *all* our actions if we want to alleviate the problems we see around us, not just when we vote or write a cheque for charity. Where we buy our food, the kind of career we choose, where we invest our money, the outreach priorities of our parish or congregation, where our union's pension fund puts its money—these decisions of daily life, multiplied by the decisions made by many other people and groups, have a dramatic impact. They either reinforce the direction in which our society and economy are heading now, or they fertilize the seeds of new life which this book has described—and many similar seeds of hope not mentioned in these pages.

"Do we want to be a nation of economic units in which whoever survives, survives, and those who can't, go under?" asks United Church minister and community organizer Susan Eagle of London, Ontario. "We sometimes forget there are choices to make. That's my reading of the gospel—a challenge and an invitation to find ways to live in community. God offers us an alternative."

Amen!

Afterword

CYNTHIA PATTERSON

In Sienna, Italy, the original Municipal Building occupies one side of the remarkable central square. On the third floor of this building, fifteenth-century frescoes, though flaked and faded, convey two distinct messages. As you enter a large room, you face the mural depicting "Bad Government." Turning round, you see its companion piece, "Good Government."

The former shows warring horsemen, stragglers on roadsides, drunkards, houses being plundered, women and children driven from their dwellings, murders. The countryside is burning, torn and littered with corpses. A few metres away a different world order is presented: healthy and happy children play at outdoor games, troubadours pluck their instruments as villagers dance, the windows of well-tended homes show inviting scenes of domesticity. Spinners, weavers, glass-blowers and others work at their crafts. Travellers with pack-laden horses hail their fellow citizens with articles for purchase. Trim ships sail the seas. Fields are filled with ripened crops. Hay stacks and brimming sacks show an abundant harvest is under way.

Good government, bad government: the effects of each were evident five hundred years ago to a Siennese painter and the city state which engaged him. They are just as evident today. One brings poverty, unemployment, homelessness, crime, militarism and degradation of the environment. The other brings peace and plenty, the dignity of work, stewardship of the land, the security necessary for agriculture, for the flourishing of arts and crafts, and fair trade.

Good government, bad government: the power of these aged frescoes lies in the deep truth they relate: the government of our nations, the government of our economies, the government of our communities, the government of our households and the government of our hearts—all are inextricably interwoven. The relations of interdependence which permit an ecosystem to thrive, or to fail when violated, are as fundamental to society as to nature. Change one part, and you affect the whole.

"It's a Wonderful Life"

Film-maker Frank Capra delivered the same message in his 1940 classic, "It's a Wonderful Life." As the hero, George Bailey (James Stewart), contemplates suicide, his guardian angel (an unlikely plump figure awaiting his wings) shows him what would have become of his town, his neighbours, friends and family, had he never been born. Although delivered in the idiom of the twentieth century, the images parallel the Siennese frescoes.

Bailey's constant work and efforts, rooted in the values of community, justice, mutuality and love, had for years and against all odds kept a thin but effective line of defence against the designs of the local capitalist-industrialist (played by Lionel Barrymore). Without Bailey, this figure's greed and lust for power go unchecked and he comes to dominate every aspect of the town's life and that of its inhabitants. Main Street is no longer a quiet, civil place where pleasantries are exchanged and people walk in the park. Gone is the Building and Loan Society, the co-operative venture initiated by Bailey's father and directed by Bailey, which made well-built, affordable housing for the town's working people. Instead, Main Street is a flashy strip where neon signs beckon an aimless and dissolute population to casinos, bars and nude revues. Further along, away from the lights, pimps and prostitutes loiter outside pawn shops as drunks lurch along the sidewalk. Cars speed by. Fights break out. Behind the town sprawls a slum, also owned by the capitalist-industrialist character. People known by Bailey as happy, productive and fulfilled are, in this alternative reality, out for themselves, mean and aggressive. Others have been utterly marginalized, the victims of alcoholism or oppression.

Frank Capra's film contrasts co-operation with competition, community with isolation, justice with injustice, generosity with greed, compassion with cruelty, creativity with destruction, love with hate. As in the Siennese frescoes, the choices of people, choices for the good or bad government of our hearts and minds, are shown to affect everyone and everything around us.

"Hard Times"

Between Sienna in the fifteenth century and Hollywood in the twentieth, we find Charles Dickens in mid-nineteenth-century industrial England. The novel "Hard Times," though less well-known than other works by Dickens, probably has more to say to the contemporary reader than do his popular classics. Written in 1854, this book sets out the creed of materialism and utilitarianism as represented by the fact-obsessed manufacturer, Mr. Gradgrind: "What you couldn't state in figures, or show to be purchasable in the cheapest market and saleable in the dearest, was not, and never should be, world without end, Amen."

Gradgrind's worldview is unwittingly challenged in the person of Sissy Jupe, a child abandoned when a visiting circus leaves town. Gradgrind's attempts to instruct Sissy in the iron logic of his beliefs and values are met with a response schooled by faith and love. When asked to state the first principal of the science of Political Economy, Sissy unhesitatingly replies, "To do unto others as I would they should do unto to me." She refers to National Prosperity as *"Natural* Prosperity," and says she is quite unable to answer the question as to whether she lives in a "prosperous nation . . . a thriving state," because, "I couldn't know whether it was a prosperous nation or not, unless I knew who had got the money, and whether any of it was mine."

While Gradgrind imposes the injunction to "never wonder" on his children, Sissy persists in her "fantastic hope." Gradgrind runs his household, his mill and Coketown, the city which he represents as a Member of Parliament, on the basis of economic fact. So divorced is his concept of the economy from the needs of people and community that Dickens likens Gradgrind to an astrologer attempting to study the stars from the interior of a windowless room. Again, the choices are clear for Dickens' readers: to follow Sissy's "fantastic hope" that economic activity need not exclude dignity and justice, or to remain imprisoned in Coketown's satanic mills.

As Janet Somerville reminds us in her Introduction, "In every generation, an economic exodus, like the one Moses began in his time, is both possible and necessary." People in each generation must choose whether or not to be part of that "exodus" leading to what Somerville calls a "redeemed economy." In our time, as this volume of essays compellingly shows, community economic development is a key part of this choice and this journey.

Yet it is precisely this issue of choices from which many shy away today. So widespread is the refusal even to acknowledge choices, not only among individuals, but among the media, politicians, industry and some representatives of the churches, that an acronym to describe the phenomena has come into use: TINA— There Is No Alternative.

The Economy is a Faith Issue

Why are we choosing to see ourselves as being without choices? Describing social sin and exploring the current state of what he calls "minimal consciousness," Kevin Arsenault writes in Chapter 3 that "when people are plunged into a life of fear and misery by economic systems that deny them freedom and dignity, their capacity for creative human development is diminished. Human suffering perpetuates despair, violence, and unhappiness." As Christians, we are called to reject the despair implicit in believing that there are no choices. As Christians, we are called to articulate the hope that arises from our faith, and to give shape and substance to the values we say we believe in. Involvement with community economic development is a powerful, practical, faithful response to the TINA syndrome.

To choose the way of CED is to act on the biblical imperative to love your neighbour by participating in "a neighbourly economy," where there are no losers, including the environment. As anyone who has ever been part of a co-operative or community undertaking will testify, the experience is spiritually transforming.

The authors of this volume of essays, however, go beyond setting out the challenges and choices. Seasoned community development practitioners and observers, they provide us with case studies that illustrate clear lessons and guideposts.

The foundation of this volume's teachings is that the economy is a faith issue. Fr. José María Arizmendiarrieta, a founder of Mondragon, the impressive Basque co-operative, stated this truth in uncompromising terms: "If the gospel does not apply to the economy, then to what does it apply?" The pursuit and creation of a just economy is therefore a requirement of living out that faith.

But those whose faith impels them to seek economic and social justice are not always supported by the churches, parishes and administrators they serve. The importance of this difficult lesson cannot be overstated. Allan Reeve's "economic ministry" initially had plenty of detractors who "argued that what Reeve was doing was social work or business development, not ministry." Allan Reeve's experience is lamentably common among Christian justice workers. The economic analysis implicit or explicit in faith-based CED is frequently criticized, even silenced, by corporate interests occupying the pews. Canada's ecclesiastical landscape—and its margins—are littered with hurt, angry, embittered and cynical people, ordained and laity, who have been undermined, muzzled and rejected by the church (of whatever denomination). Ways must be found to support the efforts of justice workers within the church, as well as in society.

The best source of support for economic justice work is the Scriptures themselves. A clear lesson from the stories in this volume is that the Scriptures are a powerful impetus to CED, and CED which remains rooted in the Scriptures will have the strength and constancy of vision to withstand the problems and temptations inevitably associated with business activities as they emerge, grow and change structurally. When the heart and mind hold fast to the source, purity of purpose will continue to guide the direction taken by the hands and feet. This is what distinguishes Christian CED from secular initiatives. This is what should protect faith-based CED from forgetting or abandoning its original mission, as have many community institutions (for example, some credit unions, buyers' co-ops, and even churches).

Faith allows those involved in CED to maintain the harmony and balance essential to a just success. The secret of Mondragon, according to Fr. Greg MacLeod, is not just technological know-how and access to capital: "The answer is found in a category better known as a value system . . . . It is about choosing one way of life over another." The will and decision to do this, to choose one way and to remain constant to that choice, depend on the individuals and communities involved. Faith must be combined with the right abilities, however. Fr. MacLeod observes of New Dawn Enterprises and other CED undertakings, "Technical ability without moral purpose will not lead anywhere. Moral purpose without technical ability is incapable of getting anything done."

A further lesson is the importance of working co-operatively, the simple and powerful principle that more can be accomplished by people working together than by people working on their own or against one another. This emphasis on creating community to affect economic and social change is a hallmark of CED. The stories in this book certainly testify to that, with regard both to the internal organization of a group and the ways in which groups relate to one another. From the co-operatives of the Evangeline region in P.E.I., to Mondragon in the Basque region of Spain, the principle remains consistent: in Fr. MacLeod's words, "Alone, each person is weak, but united as a group they become strong." The women who blocked the removal of equipment from the Scotia Rope plant came from four different denominations. The Edmonton Recycling Society was jointly formed by the Mennonite Central Committee (MCC) and Citizens for Public Justice. Kagiwiosa Manomin, the First Nation co-operative which harvests, roasts and sells wild rice, benefited at different stages from MCC advocacy work, technical and financial expertise; from Lutheran and Catholic European trade networks; and from timely loans from the church-based Canadian Alternative Investment Co-operative. The various CED loan funds are, for the most part, themselves the outcome of interdenominational efforts, enhanced by investments from secular foundations and associations.

The significance of culture for CED is a more subtle, but equally powerful lesson. A commitment to culture goes hand in hand with a commitment to place. A commitment to place means a commitment to a local economy, specifically a sustainable economy which respects the environment and plans for future generations.

The Anishinaabe people recognized that the survival of their culture depended on some measure of economic sovereignty. As Andrew Chapeskie puts it, "If you don't have control over your economic destiny, then you have control over nothing." Reclaiming their traditional relationship with manomin, and maintaining the integrity of that relationship by careful choices of harvesting and roasting methods, led to a sense of renewal for the elders and the welcome realization of employment for younger people. For the Anishinaabe, culture means a right relationship not only with manomin, but with all Creation.

The Basques connected culture and place when they made the slogan of Mondragon's credit union "Savings or Suitcases." The phrase bluntly stated the truth about the implications of where and how people choose to invest their money: in local savings for local jobs or in businesses in Madrid and elsewhere. Investing early in teaching Basque in primary schools was Mondragon's way of strengthening culture, which in turn strengthened commitment to place and the local economy.

Culture and a sense of place were the compelling reasons that Cape Bretoners took over the Scotia Rope plant, rather than follow so many other Atlantic Canadians "down the road" to jobs in Upper or Western Canada. The reality is that most people want to live and work in the place they regard as home, whether that be an outport of Newfoundland, a prairie hamlet or an island in the far north. The economic dislocation afflicting so many Canadians today alienates individuals, destroys communities and contributes significantly to urban homelessness. One of the antidotes to economic dislocation is CED. CED celebrates culture, enhances communities and honours place by growing local economies.

The Need for Structures

We've taken a look at some of the principles of CED. As Greg MacLeod reminds us, however, "Principles have to be embodied in structures." The stories in this volume also provide lessons about structures.

The co-operative is the structure favoured by most of the CED workplaces described in this book. A little tinkering is sometimes necessary to accommodate particular circumstances, but the basic concept remains. While New Dawn looks on paper more like a conventional corporation, its philosophy is unequivocally co-operative: one-vote-per-member and all profits reinvested for community purposes. The Wabigoon Lake First Nation chose a co-operative structure as the legal form of its wild rice business because it was the best compromise with traditional aboriginal ways available within Canada's current laws. These Anishinaabe create the space they need within their worker co-op, Kagiwiosa Manomin, to incorporate traditional wild-crafting relationships, organized communally around extended family groups.

Successful CED requires more than a good idea, willing hands, and a legal structure: fledgling enterprises need access to both financial and human resources. Because these are essential to every new undertaking, many CED organizations have realized the importance of meeting these needs internally, or at least by association. This calls for the creation of structures within structures, or inter-connected structures.

The precise ways of legally relating investment capital to new CED initiatives or to a larger administrative body may differ, but the goal is the same: to provide loans (and sometimes grants) to promising enterprises that likely would be turned down by mainstream financial institutions. Mondragon, New Dawn and CODA have each set up sister structures to meet this goal, whether with an actual bank or a holding company.

Several churches and foundations not involved in the operational aspects of CED have nevertheless recognized that access to capital is the greatest obstacle to development efforts. Their response has been to gather investment funds in specifically designated structures, usually separate but associated, and to lend that money to CED enterprises. Such loans may range from relatively small amounts (for example, the Anglican Community Development Fund lends up to $2,500) to the larger credit possibilities provided by the Montreal Community Loan Association ($15,000).

Structures both formal and informal, staffed by both paid and voluntary individuals, have been developed by co-operatives and CED organizations to meet human resource needs. These range from educational programs to counselling services. The essays in this book show education to be an integral part of many CED undertakings. Education is provided not only in specific technical skills, but in personal development, business planning and the managing of co-operatives. In addition to on-the-job training programs, work-study terms and specialized in-house courses, Mondragon set up the League of Education and Culture, which includes thirteen different education centres. The Edmonton Recycling Society's educational offerings, though on a more modest scale, are no less important to the success of the workplace.

Another educational component critical, not only to the financial, but to the organizational well-being of a CED project, is the mentoring system. Most of the lending organizations referred to in this book—SEED Winnipeg, Community Opportunities Development Association (CODA), the Mennonite Economic Development Association, and the Montreal Community Loan Association, to name just a few—match volunteer mentors with new CED projects as an essential counterpart to financial assistance. Once again, the spirit transforms everyone involved as mentors realize they learn at least as much as they teach.

Organizations may also provide counselling services that contribute to the strength and health of the workplace. The Edmonton Recycling Society's decision to make a Lutheran pastor available to employees at the work site three times a week, and to engage a psychologist as needed for employees or their families, is based on a commitment to wellness and to providing a family-like atmosphere of support. ("Trekkies" may remember the important role played by counsellor Troy on the Starship Enterprise!)

A structural feature of many of the CED examples cited in this book, such as the York Business Centre or Toronto Community Ventures, is that new ventures are strengthened when their owners work in clusters, sharing administration, physical space, equipment, and so forth. Quite apart from the practical and financial advantages, this neighbourly approach generates a synergy of creativity and enthusiasm that translates into a joyful business success. Think of the Evangeline region of P.E.I.: although its co-operative enterprises run independently of one another, their mutually strengthening presence has resulted in such growth that the area is known as the "co-op capital" of North America.

What is good for CED locally and regionally is also helpful nationally and internationally. Purpose is maintained and business is strengthened when dealing with individuals and organizations that share common principles and goals. Fair-trade organizations such as Oxfam's Bridgehead in Canada, the Swiss OS-3, or GEPA in Germany seek out co-operatives in all parts of the world as their business partners. These organizations are themselves part of the International Federation of Alternative Trade, committed to establish fair-trade practices with marginalized peoples.

The Challenges That Remain

If CED can do so much, why is there not more of it?

The greatest drawback is still access to capital. Yet the deeper struggle is not for the dollar, but for the soul. It is to re-kindle the faith of people so that they truly believe that there are choices, and to strengthen that faith so that action is consistent with belief.

The challenge to choose has been, as outlined earlier, always with us. But there is a fundamental difference between the results of choices made in the late-twentieth century with choices of fifteenth-century Italy, nineteenth-century England or mid-twentieth-century America. That difference is one of scale. The colonization of the planet by imperial powers was indeed an early form of globalization. But this "second globalization" by transnational corporations is more powerful, more rapid and potentially far more devastating.

Technological change means that the repercussions of current choices have a magnitude and an immediacy never before possible on the planet. Mobility of capital means that virtually no nation is isolated from the effects of corporations seeking profit at any cost. "They want the whole world in their hands," sums up Doug Smith, Winnipeg historian, columnist and activist.

The latest manifestation of the corporate will to control is the Multilateral Agreement on Investment—the MAI. Negotiated in secret by the twenty-seven members of the Organization for Economic Co-operation and Development (OECD) for over two years before draft contents were leaked, the MAI seeks to establish an international, legally binding "charter of rights for corporations," as Maude Barlow and Tony Clarke of the Council of Canadians say.

The terms of the MAI would be significantly broader than those of the North American Free Trade Agreement, and the geographic application ultimately would be global. (The OECD has been clear that once its own members have signed on, the developing world would be strongly encouraged to fall into line.) The implications of such a trade deal would be devastating for the environment, human rights, national sovereignty, and social and economic justice. It is ironic that in the very year the world marks the fiftieth anniversary of the United Nations' Declaration of Human Rights and Freedoms—1998—the corporations and governments of the richest part of the world are intent on activities that will further undermine what little gain has been made on those goals.

CED, as well as government regional development initiatives, could be directly challenged by the MAI in a number of ways. For example, the terms of the trade agreement would require public enterprises "to act solely in accordance with commercial considerations," thus making social goals, intended for the public good, illegal and subject to legal action. Another casualty would be the "buy locally" policy that many municipalities and provincial governments choose to exercise. Procurement practices at all levels of government would be subject to the articles of the MAI. No local, regional or domestic product or service could be given special consideration because the "most favoured nation" article insists that all foreign corporations be treated the same as domestic companies.

Dismaying as the consequences of the MAI would be for the hopes of a just society, the effects on the natural world, on Creation, could be disastrous. Proponents of the MAI recognize no limits to growth, whatever the polished public-relations statements might say. The evidence is all around us. The earth cannot bear further abuse.

Confronted by this new, pervasive globalization, the choice each one of us must make is fundamental: "I set before you life and death . . . ." Observing that "economics has been elevated to the level of a religion in our society," community organizer Joan Kuyek urges us to "reclaim and re-name economics for ourselves." To reclaim the economy means to engage directly with the holders of wealth and power. As Dickens' Sissy Jupe said, "I couldn't know whether it was a prosperous nation or not, unless I knew who had got the money, and whether any of it was mine." Millions of people, most of them children like Sissy Jupe, know that according to the criteria of just sharing of wealth and power, we cannot say we have a prosperous nation, nor a prosperous planet.

To reclaim the economy also means reclaiming our faith. We need to state boldly that our faith resides in a theology of hope, of joy and of justice. Our faith does not reside in the marketplace. We need to make this statement inside our churches as well as in the world. Murray MacAdam points out that "the church is in a unique and potentially powerful position to challenge the secular gospel drummed into us daily about the economy." We need to take up that challenge, as individuals and as institutions. The task is not a small one. As Allan Reeve and countless others know, many church members and church administrators are themselves mesmerized by the mantras of "debt," "deficit," "globalization" and the inevitability of "competition." Jennifer Henry of the Ecumenical Coalition for Economic Justice accurately sets out the dilemma: "We need to look at how the 'justice' church can come to terms with the 'bond-holder' church." The inconsistencies between what we say and what we do are obvious. Mennonite Paul Born puts it this way: "The church recognizes the importance of work and economic development in developing countries. Why is it so silent about CED in Canada?" The 1997 statement by Canadian church leaders reminds church, government and society that "all economic choices are ultimately moral choices." The statement is titled *Restless for the Reign of God.* Just how restless are we?

Central to moving through and beyond the contradictions is the recognition and acknowledgement by all concerned that none of the old models is working. As Fr. MacLeod asserts, "Communism and capitalism are irrelevant words." If the old models are not working, what do we do? Where do we go? Is there yet a new model? If so, what does it look like? In order to be faithful and relevant in the late twentieth century, the churches are called to engage with these profound and difficult questions. If our faith gives us courage to reject the "TINA" syndrome, can we name the alternatives?

The most compelling challenge for CED, according to Eric Shragge, is to come up with new models, to provide "a credible alternative to the prevailing conservative view of the economy." This is not only a challenge for CED. Citizens' groups, environmental groups, justice workers, some people within some churches, the political left—the broad progressive movement throughout the world—are grappling with the same challenge. We've done some great analysis of the problems. What do the solutions look like?

Various terms are used to describe the model we'd like to see. John Kenneth Galbraith calls it "the good society." Others speak of "civil society." The Council of Canadians has put together "A Citizens' Agenda." People of faith speak of the "reign of God." While the names may differ, the constant is a deep concern for justice, including justice for the Creation.

But how do we get there? As yet, no step-by-step treatise has been written, no inspiring manifesto has emerged. Neither the

Adam Smith nor the Karl Marx of our time has been revealed. We cannot seek refuge in ideology.

The fact is, no one and no single organization can draw a map of a new, just tomorrow. Yet it is also a fact that many individuals, organizations and corporations—sometimes with benefit of charitable status and government co-operation—are drawing a map to quite another sort of tomorrow, one that looks a lot like the mural of "Bad Government" in Sienna.

This is why the challenge to the churches is so strong, so immediate and so important. Three activities are essential to inspiring people with the courage and determination to take their part in the creation of a just world. The churches have both the experience and the faith foundation required to enter into these three.

The first task is to *witness,* to declare boldly and publicly that the present system is not working and is wrongfully motivated.

The second is to help to *articulate the new vision,* to remind people of the promised reign of God, and to help them believe that justice is possible.

> *Endow the king with your justice, O God . . . .*
> *He will judge your people in righteousness,*
> *your afflicted ones with justice.*
> *The mountains will bring prosperity to the people,*
> *the hills the fruit of righteousness.*
> *. . . .*
> *He will endure as long as the sun,*
> *as long as the moon, through all generations.*
> *He will be like rain falling on a mown field,*
> *like showers watering the earth.*
> *In his days the righteous will flourish;*
> *prosperity will abound till the moon is no more.*
> *. . . .*
> *For he will deliver the needy who cry out,*
> *the afflicted who have no one to help.*
> *He will take pity on the weak and the needy*
> *and save the needy from death.*
> *He will rescue them from oppression and violence.*

. . . .

Let grain abound throughout the land;
on the tops of the hills may it sway,
Let its fruit flourish like Lebanon;
let it thrive like the grass of the field.

. . . .

All nations will be blessed through him,
and they will call him blessed.

Psalm 72

The third is perhaps the most faithful task: to *walk into the darkness without fear.* That is part of what is required of us at this time in history. We don't have the answers. We can sketch in some of the picture, and CED is an important part of the emerging image, but we can't see the whole thing. So we must enter the darkness, trusting the darkness.

Think of watching a photograph emerge from a chemical bath in a darkroom. First, nothing but blackness; then, patches of grey slide across the face of the dark; form begins dimly to take shape; finally, a full and detailed image emerges.

Or imagine this: a blindingly bright day in February; the white of the snow, and the blue of the sky. When you walk into the unlit woodshed you cannot see a thing. You grasp a wheelbarrow to steady yourself, make your way along the row of tools. You relax. Your pupils dilate. Slowly, quietly, from darkness into light, slip row upon row of carefully stacked maple, old cherry, yellow birch, fir and spruce.

Light out of darkness; form out of the void; order out of chaos. It sounds a little like Creation, doesn't it?

We don't have to know everything to begin the journey. We must be confident in the renewal of our minds and "know this love that surpasses knowledge" (Ephesians 3:19). We must be willing to move forward, trusting that we will find our way. "For now we see through a glass darkly, but then shall we see face to face" (1 Corinthians 13:12).

Our ability to be co-creators of a just world is limited only by our imagination and our small faith. And these need not be limited:

Now unto him who is able to do immeasurably more than all we ask or imagine, according to his power that is at work within us, to him be glory in the church and in Christ Jesus throughout all generations.

Ephesians 3:20

People of faith know how to do this. We need to remind ourselves of that faithful ability and share it with others.

People of faith and our churches need to resume our rightful place in the debate about the kind of world we should have, and what we want to leave to future generations.

Resources

Books

Douglas, David. *Community Economic Development in Canada*. 2 volumes. Toront: McGraw-Hill Ryerson, 1994 and 1995. A comprehensive look at CED across Canada, written by a variety of CED organizers and researchers and often from an academic perspective. Each chapter focuses on a particular region or aspect of CED.

Ellmen, Eugene. *The 1997 Canadian Ethical Money Guide*. Toronto: James Lorimer, 1996. If you've asked yourself, What can I do with my money to make the world a better place? then this book is for you. This book shows you how to make ethical investments through ethical mutual funds, labour-sponsored funds, credit unions and in other ways. Community loan funds which promote CED are also listed. Helpful for investors large and small.

Kuyek, Joan. *Fighting For Hope: Organizing to Realize Our Dreams*. Montreal: Black Rose Books, 1990. A book which comes at the "big issues" of economic and political power in a refreshingly down-to-earth style, reflecting the author's long experience of grassroots organizing. Covers social analysis, the structures of power, and strategies for change, and includes a chapter on reclaiming economics.

Perry, Stewart E. *Reinventing the Local Economy: What Ten Canadian Initiatives Can Teach Us about Building Creative, Inclusive and Sustainable Communities*. Vernon, B.C.: Centre for Community Enterprise, 1994. Two experts (Mike Lewis was co-author) present ten examples of community economic action from one end of Canada to the other. The examples vary widely and the authors provide an honest assessment of the positive and negative aspects of CED.

Quarter, Jack. *Building a Community Controlled Economy: The Evangeline Co-operative.* Toronto: University of Toronto Press, 1996.

Quarter, Jack. *Canada's Social Economy.* Toronto: James Lorimer, 1992. Did you know that about one in every seven Canadian jobs is found in our "social economy"—the large non-profit sector of the economy? This book outlines the importance of co-operatives, non-profits and other community enterprises.

Roberts, Wayne and Susan Brandum. *Get A Life!* Toronto: Get A Life Publishing House, 1995. An inspirational, irreverent and thoroughly entertaining book, full of ideas and projects for earning a living—and simply living—in a way that protects the Creation and respects human values. Includes ideas both for individual action and for broader economic development.

Shragge, Eric. *Community Economic Development: In Search of Empowerment.* Montreal: Black Rose Books, 1997. An updated version of Shragge's earlier book of the same title. Makes the point that CED must be much more than a local economic strategy: it must include broader social and political goals that empower people. Profiles various CED ventures, including some mentioned in this book, such as New Dawn, West End Community Ventures and the Montreal Community Loan Association.

Social Investment Organization. *Mobilizing Local Capital: A CED Investment Manual.* Available from the SIO, 366 Adelaide St. East, Suite 447, Toronto, Ont. M5A 3X9. Has ideas to help groups across Canada establish financing strategies for CED initiatives. Contains examples of successful projects and programs from across Canada.

World Vision. *Churches at Work in the Community: Strategies to Improve Local Job Opportunities.* An American book which shows how church and community groups, in partnership with business and local government, can help provide work for low-income, hard-to-employ people. Covers help with searching for a job, mentoring, local job training and financing, including community loan funds. The book's U.S. context limits its relevance for Canadians, but there is still much that is instructive. Available from CCE Publications, P.O. Box 1161, Station A, Port Alberni, B.C. V9Y 9Z9. Phone 1-888-255-6779.

Publications

Making Waves. Canada's community economic development quarterly. Published by the Centre for Community Enterprise. Subscriptions from CCE Publications, P.O. Box 1161, Station A, Port Alberni, B.C. V9Y 9Z9. Phone 1-888-255-6779.

Sustainable Times. A peppy quarterly "newsmagazine about solutions" published by CUSO and the Halifax Initiative. Subscriptions from CUSO, 1657 Barrington St., #508, Halifax, N.S. B3J 2A1.

Organizations

Ecumenical Coalition for Economic Justice (ECEJ). Through research, education and political action, this feisty church-backed group spearheads a range of efforts for economic justice. The coalition is backed by the Anglican, Roman Catholic, Lutheran, Presbyterian and United Churches. Through the coalition, the churches remind policy-makers, church people and the public that economic life is related to the values we hold.

Several hundred people in 20 communities across Canada are taking part in ECEJ's Faith and Justice Training Project, intensive educational workshops designed to equip people with the skills needed to promote a moral economy. The Coalition also publishes an action kit for promoting the *Alternative Federal Budget.* ECEJ, 947 Queen St. E., Toronto, Ont. M4M 1J9. Phone: (416) 462-1613; fax (416) 463-5569. E-mail address: ccej@accessv.com

Canadian Centre for Policy Alternatives. Along with individuals and other groups, this Ottawa-based organization promotes economic policies geared to the needs of ordinary Canadians and to democratic economic development. Promotes the *Alternative Federal Budget.* Canadian Centre for Policy Alternatives, 251 Laurier Ave. W., Suite 804, Ottawa, Ont. K1P 5J6. Website: www.policyalternatives.ca

Citizens for Public Justice. A national Christian advocacy organization promoting justice and compassion in Canadian public affairs, including a more humane economy. CPJ, 229 College St., #311, Toronto, Ont. M5T 1R4. Phone: 1-800-667-8046. Website: www.web.net/~cpj

CED Organizations

Anglican Community Development Fund. Supports low-income people starting small businesses with small loans and mentoring support. Contact the directors through the Anglican Diocese of Toronto. Phone: (416) 363-6021.

BCA Holdings. A community-based venture capital corporation working to improve the economy of Cape Breton Island through investments in small businesses. BCA Holdings, P.O. Box 1201, 292 Charlotte St., Sydney, N.S. B1P 6J9. Phone: (902) 539-1777.

Canadian Alternative Investment Co-op. The co-op helps finance socially beneficial Canadian projects through mortgages, loans and equity investments. Membership is limited to registered Canadian charities incorporated in Canada. New members who agree with CAIC's values and goals are welcome. Canadian Alternative Investment Co-op, 146 Laird Drive, Suite 106, Toronto, Ont. M4G 3V7. Phone/fax: (416) 467-7797.

Community Business Resource Centre. Provides training and other resources for self-employment, special programs for new Canadians, and help for neighbourhood economic development. Community Business Resource Centre, 145 Front St. E., Toronto, Ont. M5A 1E3. Phone: (416) 415-2370. Website: www.cbrc.com

Community Opportunities Development Association (CODA). A broad-based economic development agency in the Cambridge-Kitchener-Waterloo area of Ontario. CODA specializes in self-employment training for people on welfare and in various forms of support for new entrepreneurs. The agency launched the SEED Fund, a fund for community loans. CODA, 35 Dickson St., Cambridge, Ont. N1R 7A8. Phone (519) 623-9380.

Edmonton Recycling Society. 1631-80 St., Edmonton, Alta. T5B QN3. Phone: (403) 471-0071; fax: 479-7700.

Kagiwiosa Manomin. Their rice is available in Ontario from the Ontario Federation of Food Co-ops or can be ordered directly from Kagiwiosa Manomin Inc., Wabigoon Lake Band #27, Site 112, Box 13, Dinorwic, Ont. P0V 1P0. Phone: (807) 938-6927. Email: manomin@dryden.lakeheadu.ca

Montreal Community Loan Association. An innovative community organization which uses its capital to provide low-cost loans to residents and community businesses in low-income areas of Montreal. Phone: (514) 844-9882, E-mail: ACEM@libertel.montreal.qc.ca.

Ontario Worker Co-op Federation. Promotes the development of new worker co-ops. OWCF, 83 Grove St., Guelph, Ont. N1E 2W6. Phone/fax: (519) 766-0082.

Riverdale Economic Ministry. Promotes the CED business model in Toronto's low-income South Riverdale neighbourhood and encourages church support for CED. Works closely with Toronto Community Ventures, a network of CED businesses in South Riverdale. Riverdale Economic Ministry, 158 Eastern Ave., Toronto, Ont. M5A 4C4. Phone: (416) 955-0855.

Winnipeg CED Network & Resource Group. A group of organizations and individuals which promote CED in Winnipeg. Winnipeg CED Network & Resource Group, 108-424 Logan Ave., Winnipeg, MB. R3A 0R4. Phone: (204)947-6940.

Women and Rural Economic Development. Provides business training for rural women, loans, and resources for women's business networks. Women and Rural Economic Development, 379 Huron St., Stratford, Ont. N5A 5T6. Website: www.sentex.net/~wred

Québec, Canada
1998